Emerging Awakening—A Faith Quake

Emerging Awakening—A Faith Quake

Revival Is Rising in the Emerging Church

Wayne Detzler

Foreword by
Justin Kendrick

WIPF & STOCK · Eugene, Oregon

EMERGING AWAKENING—A FAITH QUAKE
Revival is Rising in the Emerging Church

Copyright © 2013 Wayne Detzler. All rights reserved. Except for brief quotations in critical publications or reviews, no part of this book may be reproduced in any manner without prior written permission from the publisher. Write: Permissions, Wipf and Stock Publishers, 199 W. 8th Ave., Suite 3, Eugene, OR 97401.

Wipf & Stock
An Imprint of Wipf and Stock Publishers
199 W. 8th Ave., Suite 3
Eugene, OR 97401

www.wipfandstock.com

ISBN 13: 978-1-61097-987-0

Manufactured in the U.S.A.

*To
My grandchildren,
Nick and Erika Khamarji, Katrina Samuelson,
Matthew Detzler, Samuel Detzler, and Sara Detzler
As they carry the gospel into a new generation,
the Millennial generation.*

Contents

Foreword by Justin Kendrick | *ix*
Author's Preface | *xiii*

    Introduction—To Church or Not to Church | 1
1   Revival Happens | 9
2   Core Values of the Emerging Church | 29
3   Vertical Worship—God Centered | 53
4   Living Belief—No Dead Dogmas | 74
5   Why the Church is Emerging | 93
6   Facing Forward—Not Backward | 111
7   Emerging Revival—Fact or Fantasy? | 129

Bibliography | *139*

Foreword

A FEW YEARS AGO I was sitting in a waiting room dealing with an issue for my child's insurance. It was a normal day. Nothing flashy. Nothing special. After a few minutes a young lady about my age sat down next to me. We both awkwardly shuffled in our seats until she leaned over and introduced herself. She cordially asked me my name, and soon we were talking about what I do for work. I shared about Jesus. I didn't preach a sermon. I just spoke out of who I am. Then I turned the tables on her and asked about her life.

"Well, actually," she replied with a subtle smile on her face, "I'm a stripper."

Now that doesn't happen every day.

You learn a lot about yourself by the way you respond to the "I'm a stripper" comment. I wasn't sure what the best response was, so I decided to go with my gut. I told her that God had a better story for her, and that she didn't have to take off her clothes to feel valued. She defended her occupation, saying she liked the attention and the money helped pay for college. The conversation ended as I shared about me and my wife's relationship and how we had waited to have sex until after we were married. The girl didn't believe me. She tried to get me to tell her it wasn't true. Finally, tears started to well up in her eyes.

"I wish I waited," she said quietly.

The church is at a crossroads in history. God never changes, but he uses various means to wake up his sleeping bride and reignite passion for his eternal purposes. The truth is that whether we like it or not, we are sitting next to the stripper. She's bold, she's proud, and inwardly she's screaming for hope and healing.

The church can do a few things in this moment. We can ignore her and go about our normal routines, acting like everything is lovely while an entire generation runs farther and farther from God. This has been the strategy of some. They've acted like old methods will work on a new generation, assuming kids who grew up learning they can't trust their parents will blindly trust spiritual leaders and continue to participate in the Christian machine. It's not working. They aren't coming.

We can acknowledge her, welcome her in, and pretend the stripper is just your healthy, young daughter. This may work for a little while, until she becomes desperately tired of the show and leaves the church claiming no one cares and everyone wears a mask. This in turn drives her deeper into the arms of a welcoming world.

If we genuinely want the love of Jesus to touch her soul we must humbly, courageously embrace her and introduce her to the Jesus who heals her heart and walks with her to freedom. We can't be shocked, scared, or surprised by her sin. We can't condemn her or act like the wounds she carries are too deep to heal. In Luke 5 Jesus meets a man dying of leprosy. The man throws his decaying body at the feet of Jesus and says, "Lord if you're willing you can make me clean." Right now, across the landscape of the church, God is raising up a generation that will take the words of Jesus to the lepers and the strippers. His response is the same today as it was two thousand years ago. He is willing. Be cleansed.

The emerging church is a complex and multi-layered phenomenon reshaping the way people practice their faith across the globe. Like all moves of God, there is good and bad. It seems in our time, God is reawakening his people to a few central truths. Many emerging leaders are preaching a gospel that puts Jesus at the center of our lives and paints Christianity as a life-system and not simply a belief system. Gone are the days when Christians can attend church on Sunday and move on with the week. God is not simply the top priority as if we could check him off the list and move to the next thing. He is the fuel behind all of life's decisions.

People are rediscovering the Jesus who brings freedom in all areas of life, realizing it is holiness that makes us free and sin that makes us slaves. In a culture that champions privacy, the church is again embracing community and transparency as a model for living, doing life with others rather than simply doing "church" once a week.

The landscape is changing and we can't afford to sleep through this moment.

We must put this move of God in its historical context, realizing the picture is a lot bigger than some new music or a fresh style. We must hold to the beauty and clarity of the gospel, believing the truth found in Jesus is

Foreword

our anchor and hope. We must look out over a broken humanity and realize that at this era in history there is no room for consumers and armchair quarterbacks. We must love deeply, sacrifice often, seek humbly, and preach boldly.

We have been given a great privilege. I'm convinced that right now the opportunity to advance the gospel is the greatest in human history. Dr. Wayne Detzler has done us a great service by studying the shape this move of God is taking, and putting it in context so the impact can be maximized. Let's seek the Lord together as fathers and sons, mothers and daughters, believing God is faithful from generation to generation.

Justin Kendrick
Lead Pastor, City Church
Director, Holyfire Ministries

Author's Preface

As I WRITE THIS book controversy is swirling around the emerging church. It is fuelled to some degree by the doctrinal heresy of certain well-known pastors and preachers. Likewise there is the inevitable generational conflict, as older Christ followers fumble to understand their younger contemporaries. Finally, there is vast divergence within the emerging movement, a divergence Phyllis Tickle has discerned and described in her masterful book, *The Great Emergence: How Christianity is Changing and Why*.

For many people in my generation, the controversy is enough to stop further investigation. However, years of work as a professor and a pastor have honed my imagination and emboldened my spirit. When my generational contemporaries condemned the emerging church, I was both intrigued and incensed. This caused me to visit as many of the emerging churches as I could and build bridges of communication to the lead pastors and their pastoral assistants. As a lifelong pastor, I feel most comfortable with these faith friends.

After a prolonged search I discovered there are many biblical, powerful preachers within the emerging movement, and they are committed to search for spiritual awakening. This moved me to spread the net wider, to contact pastors in England, Europe, and Australia. It also compelled me to seek similarities with the Chinese churches, where we have discipled a new generation of leaders.

I am deeply thankful to those who have assisted. Nick Khamarji, my grandson-in-law, has connected me with the leading lights in the emerging church movement. In many cases he has provided me with video and written data to forward the search.

Through Nick I also met Justin Kendrick. As lead pastor of City Church in New Haven, Connecticut, Justin is an immediate and accessible source of invaluable material concerning the emerging church movement.

Author's Preface

He has given unstintingly of his time and energy to assist me in this project. His refreshing approach to pastoral challenges continues to thrill me.

My primary source for the English scene is Mark Detzler, my son. He serves an emerging church in the center of Bristol, England. He is also employed by a city college, which keeps him in constant touch with the millennial community.

On the continent of Europe I connected with Annelies Strupler. Annelies and her husband, Heinz, have been on the cutting edge of evangelical advance in Switzerland and across the world for many years. They actually birthed the International Christian Fellowship in Zurich, which is a model of emerging church growth for all of Europe.

Words fail me to thank my resource people in various churches. They have shared their hearts as they have described their experiences in the emerging movement. To them and to those whom they lead I owe a debt of gratitude.

Finally, I am so thankful to our daughter Dr. Carol Samuelson and her husband Scott Samuelson for providing a beautiful home here in Connecticut. It gives a peaceful place to write as well as ready access to vibrant east coast cities and universities.

Wayne Detzler
Trumbull, Connecticut
2012

Introduction—To Church or Not to Church

IN HIS RECENT BOOK, *You Lost Me*, David Kinnaman of the Barna Group exposes a yawning chasm. It gapes between young, 18–30 year-old Christians and so-called contemporary Christian churches. Their main beef is not with old-fashioned, traditional worship. It is with trendy, soft-rock, contemporary worship.

Truth be told, they are not so much turned off by the form of worship. It is the very core of preaching that ignites alienation. As a professor at a major east coast Catholic university I have a front-row seat as each year a parade of bright, inquisitive freshmen come through the door. With lamentable regularity we notice a widening gap between them and Christianity. This goes beyond a rejection of formal Christianity, both Catholic and Protestant. It is also disenchantment with evangelical Christianity. Why is this so? In a powerful article David Kinnaman, president and co-owner of the Barna Group, set down six propositions to explain the trend.[1]

First, churches seem overprotective. They profess to connect with the culture of their community, but they stifle any attempts to engage in meaningful interaction. This criticism of community action is devastating. When I tried to light a candle within the local school board in a major southern city, I was chastised by pastoral staff members in my home church.

Second, members of the Millennial or Mosaic generation experience Christianity as being intellectually shallow. They receive little or no help from evangelical churches when it comes to preparation for life-decisions. It seems as if biblical truth must be divorced from everyday life. This is the fallacy that forced Søren Kierkegaard into his existential approach to Christianity. For this Danish philosopher, Christianity is not what we do but rather who we are. Obviously, this became an offense to the hide-bound theologians of Danish Lutheranism. Is it not ironic that this question

---

1. Kinnaman, "Six Reasons."

emerges perennially? As the German historiographer Leopold von Ranke put it: "Every generation stands face-to-face with God." It is the purpose of this book to assess the relationship between Millennial young people and God, but it is not my purpose to defend previous church practices and rites.

Third, churches appear to be antagonistic to science. Since the days of Darwin Christians have fought an ongoing battle against evolution. They have perceived Darwin's view of evolution to be a slap to the very face of God. If God created the universe and all that is in it from nothing, then Darwin's *On the Origin of Species* is a lie straight from the pit of hell. Many Christians seem to have written off scientific inquiry in general and scientific experimentation in particular. They focus their venom on such issues as stem-cell research and the Human Genome Project. Young believers within the Millennial or Mosaic generation conclude that Christianity and science are like chalk and cheese—totally incompatible. Unfortunately, they deduce that Christianity has thrown out the baby with the bath water. Nearly three out of ten young people believe churches are out of step with the scientific world we live in. Almost one-quarter of young Christians claim they have been turned off by the creation-versus-evolution debate. While opposing the concepts of the origin of the species, Christians have too often rejected all scientific advances.

Fourth, young Christians find churches are simplistic and judgmental when it comes to matters of sexuality. This is especially true of young Catholic Christians. They have grown up under the tutelage of priests and nuns who are committed to sexual abstinence and opposed to artificial birth control. At the same time, many evangelical churches are so ambivalent about the subject of sex that they fail to provide appropriate teaching to young adults. When young adults become sexually active they discover their church has marginalized them, even ostracized them. According to Kinnaman's research, fully one-sixth of young Christians said they "have made mistakes and feel judged in church because of them."[2] Catholic Christians sometimes simply give up when they conclude the church's "teachings on sexuality and birth control are out of date."[3]

Fifth, young Christians wrestle with the exclusive claims of Christianity. They have grown up in a pluralistic society, which is also a secular society. The implicit message of both popular and serious culture in America is this: all truth is scientific truth. No reality exists outside the realm of time and

2. Ibid.
3. Ibid.

space. Religion is wholly mythological, so there is no right or wrong in the realm of religion. Tolerance is the best we can do. Nearly one in three believe "churches are afraid of the beliefs of other churches."[4] For this reason, many parents adopt a defensive position. They send their young people to Christian schools or simply home school them. This is based on the false viewpoint that students can be isolated from the wide world of non-Christian ideas. On a very basic level this question of Christian exclusivity exposes the power of peer pressure. Almost one in three claimed they were forced to choose between their church and their friends. Kinnaman concludes: "Today's young are the most eclectic generation in American history in terms of race, ethnicity, sexuality, religion, technological tools, and sources of authority."[5]

Sixth, the church is unfriendly to doubters. More than one in three students responded that they were not able to "ask my most pressing life question in church."[6] Almost one in four expressed doubts about the Christian faith. Furthermore, teachers will confirm that many students wrestle with serious issues of depression, alienation, even rage. None of these can be safely aired in most evangelical churches. When pressed, most churches leaders suggest trivial solutions to the deepest distress. "Just believe" is a retreat to simplistic fideism. By contrast, Jesus took doubt seriously. When John the Baptist was assailed by doubt during his final imprisonment, Jesus took time to send a powerful response (Matt 11:1–13). After the resurrection Jesus' disciples gathered in the upper room, but Thomas was absent. He was alienated by his very doubts. Jesus counteracted the doubts of Thomas by appearing to him, and Thomas was renewed in his faith (John 20:19–31).

For these reasons, many young believers turn to the emerging church. The worship is real, and the preaching is marked by authenticity. However, the evangelical establishment is not amused by this.

A retired professor I knew once warned his Bible study group: "There is a new heresy, even a cult, preying on Christians today. It is the emerging church." When I challenged this generalization, the professor was not amused. His opinion often prevails, even though many times college-age grandchildren of the church abandon worship altogether.

The mere mention of the emerging church propels some traditional theologians into a paroxysm of wrath. Emerging churches are too loud in their worship, too shallow in their preaching, and too limited in their

---

4. Ibid.
5. Ibid.
6. Ibid.

audience. They regard supporters of the emerging church, such as Scot McKnight,[7] with suspicion. Even respected, serious authors like D. A. Carson single out aberrant examples and demolish them with delight.

In his critical book, *Becoming Conversant with the Emerging Church*, D. A. Carson identifies two authors as being aberrant in their theology. They are Brian McLaren and Steven Chalke (He could have also added Rob Bell to this list). According to Carson, the key issue is epistemology, how we learn. He states that McLaren and Chalke are postmodern in their way of knowing. They reject rational foundations of truth by seeking to deconstruct the Christian faith. Faith is like beauty. It is in the eye of the beholder. Whatever one believes to be true is true.[8] This sort of deconstructionism has been applied to literature, political philosophy, and language in general. McLaren and Chalke now apply it to the very essence of our Christian faith.

Since the appearance of D. A. Carson's book, the face of the emerging church has changed. Many of the lead pastors are very sophisticated theologically, just as they are passionate preachers. They actually hold their young congregation accountable to the Scriptures, and to biblical living especially.

One further contribution to the subject of emerging churches is the landmark book by Eddie Gibbs and Ryan Bolger. They have written a comprehensive survey of the emerging churches in various cultures under the title, *Emerging Churches: Creating Christian Community in Postmodern Cultures*. They have focused their efforts on assessing the pragmatic posture of emerging churches. Very wisely, Gibbs and Bolger identify the passion of emerging churches as transforming culture, receiving strangers into community, and spending their efforts in self-sacrificing service. Eddie Gibbs has previously written encyclopedic classics such as, *I Believe in Church Growth* and *In Name Only*. Although Eddie Gibbs teaches at Fuller Theological Seminary, he represents the best of his native British, Christian scholarship. He has obviously passed on this passion to Ryan Bolger, who is a younger writer.

It is the thesis of this book that there is true revival among the emerging churches. By surveying lead pastors from the United States, Australia, the United Kingdom, and even Switzerland, I have attempted to build a picture of the rising tide of spiritual awakening. For instance, Kevin Butterfield serves in Melbourne, Australia. He dares to compare the movement among emerging churches with the revival led by Charles Finney in

---

7. McKnight, "Five Streams of the Emerging Church."
8. Carson, *Becoming Conversant*, 27.

Introduction—To Church or Not to Church

nineteenth-century America. Interestingly, Butterfield's church has found a home within the Vineyard movement. Throughout the book we will notice that emerging churches are often part of denominational structures.

On another front we met Derwin Gray, who is lead pastor of Transformation Church in Fort Mill, South Carolina. Gray is a former NFL linebacker, who now directs his drive into the building of an authentic church fellowship. He has found a home within the Christian and Missionary Alliance as he draws on the holiness influence of A. B. Simpson. After a thriving itinerant preaching ministry, Derwin Gray opened the doors of Transformation Church near metropolitan Charlotte, North Carolina. Immediately, the church drew a large congregation.

By the same token, Steven Furtick is lead pastor of Elevation Church in Charlotte, North Carolina. His pedigree is somewhat unusual. He graduated from the traditional Southern Baptist Theological Seminary in Louisville, Kentucky. When he opened the doors of Elevation Church he formally started a Southern Baptist Church. Later on we will notice how Furtick's ministry differs from other churches in the Southern Baptist Convention.

Dan Burrell is executive pastor at Life Fellowship in Huntersville, North Carolina. Arising out of the culture of southern evangelical Christianity, Life Fellowship has taken on the appearance of the emerging church. As a result, they have made a strong impact on the mushrooming population of north Charlotte.

One of the most intriguing models of the emerging church is Hillsong NYC. With roots in the Hillsong United worship movement, Carl and Laura Lentz spearheaded a creative outreach in Manhattan. It is known as Hillsong NYC. Because Millennial young people comprise such a large segment of New York population Hillsong has settled into the sweet spot of ministry.

In Bristol, England our son, Mark Detzler, recently opened the doors to Bristol City Centre Church. Again, the historical connections are influential on this ministry. With roots reaching deeply into the Reformed Baptist Tradition of Charles Haddon Spurgeon, Bristol City Centre Church weaves together strong, dynamic musical worship and deep reformed Bible teaching. It draws on the young population of students and professional people in the historic center of Bristol, a city that once responded to the revival preaching of John Wesley, George Muller, and Charles Haddon Spurgeon.

Another source for our study is the work of Justin Kendrick, lead pastor City Church in New Haven, Connecticut. The city is a model of modern sociological schizophrenia. On one hand, brilliant Yale students roam the streets with professors known worldwide for their genius. By the same token, New Haven is one of the most violent cities in Connecticut. Kendrick gained notoriety as the band Out of Hiding and Holy Fire Ministries before planting a church in the center of New Haven. Each Sunday Kendrick and his wife, Krissy, lead the band as worship rings out in a downtown arts high school theater setting. They too are connected to a mother church, Church, in nearby Hamden, Connecticut.

Josh Feay graduated from Yale Divinity School before joining the pastor staff at Black Rock Congregational Church in Fairfield, Connecticut. He leads a ministry called Sanctuary that models after the emerging church. Although their venue is the traditional Black Rock Church worship center, Sanctuary has carved out a niche for ministry to Millennials living throughout southern Connecticut. Interestingly, Sanctuary was started by Kevin Butterfield, our resource person in Australia.

An addition to our study is Sandals Church in Riverside, California. Lead pastor Matt Brown was mentored by Rick Warren, and Sandals has taken the vision to a new generation. Because of the university presences in Riverside, many students find a worship home at Sandals. Authenticity is the key for Sandals, as they state their vision of "being real with ourselves, real with God, and real with others."[9] Justin Pardee from the Sandals staff has been extremely helpful as we developed this book.

The point is this: the emerging churches no longer inhabit the lunatic fringe of Christian life. They are completely connected to other believers. In fact, one of the dominant drives is cultivating community with other believers. Never have I felt out of place or unwelcome in an emerging church worship experience.

But it is not their connectedness that we here emphasize. Rather, it is their passion for authentic faith, their resolve for revival. In his first sermon that launched weekly worship at City Church, Justin Kendrick put it this way: "City Church exists to spread the lifestyle of authentic Christianity for the glory of God and for the transformation of our city." Then he added: "Now is the time for spiritual awakening to spread across New Haven County and for the resurgence of authentic Christianity."[10]

---

9. Justin Pardee, email interview to author, January 19, 2012.
10. Kendrick, "Building Foundations."

Introduction—To Church or Not to Church

To underline the necessity for revival in modern New Haven, Kendrick quoted one of his favorite authors, the revivalist Charles Grandison Finney. Finney deduced seven signs of a society in need of revival:[11]

1. Christians lack brotherly love.
2. There is jealousy and backbiting among Christians.
3. The church looks like the world.
4. The church is wracked by scandalous sin.
5. The church is consumed with controversy.
6. The wicked succeed and scoff at the church.
7. People are careless about eternity.

This list seems eerily familiar because it overlaps with many concerns expressed by the Millennial generation, the Mosaics. As a lifelong student of revival, I have discovered the spiritual and moral breakdown of the church is a perennial occurrence. Almost always does it precede a spiritual revival. When we consider past revivals these phenomena will become abundantly clear.

Revival has consumed my study and my ministry for more than fifty years. Not only have I researched historical and contemporary revivals, but I have also participated in revival movements in America, Europe, and Asia. In fact, my doctoral dissertation plumbed the depths of a revival in Germany, known as the *Erweckung*. Let me set down some boundaries for our study of revival. Revival is not a preplanned series of meetings in a local church, although these are often called and erroneously known as "revivals." Revival is a sovereign act of God, whereby he unilaterally rejuvenates believers as they come back to spiritual life and others come to spiritual life through the process.

The question before us is this: is there true revival in the emerging church? In order to discern the nature of the emerging church, it is the intent of this author to first formulate the characteristics of revival. In this effort we shall undertake a broad historical survey of awakenings. This will yield a list of the manifestations within the church and society. Without delving into all the details of historical revivals, we shall endeavor to discern significant signs as they appear among both Christ followers and also those who do not yet

---

11. Finney, *Thoughts on Revival*, as quoted by Justin Kendrick in his sermon "Why City Church," February 19, 2012.

believe in the Lord. We shall begin with the sixteenth-century Reformation and select a series of revivals in various cultures since then.

Indeed we shall focus on six major movements: (1) the Protestant Reformation, (2) Pietism, Wesleyanism, and the Great Awakening (3) Finney, Moody, and the *Réveil* and *Erweckung*, (4) Pentecostalism and the Jesus People, and (5) the House Church Movement in China. Obviously, this study will be somewhat superficial, but I will attempt to discern characteristics common to revivals across the centuries. Then we shall apply this matrix of phenomena to the emerging church to discover whether or not it is a true revival movement.

The main body of our work is a careful comparative investigation into the life and practice of emerging churches. To ensure accuracy, we shall base our study of emerging churches on interviews with pastors in the United States, the United Kingdom, Europe, and Australia.

After surveying the marks of revival, this list will overlay the phenomena of the emerging church. Our effort is to establish whether or not the emerging church is truly a revival movement. Finally, we shall attempt a prognosis for the emerging church. What lies in the future of this dynamic movement?

1

Revival Happens

IN ORDER TO GAIN a deeper understanding of revival movements, we shall focus on five separate and very diverse revivals: (1) the Protestant Reformation, (2) pietism, Wesleyanism, and the Great Awakening (3) Finney, Moody, and the *Réveil* and *Erweckung*, (4) Pentecostalism and the Jesus People, and (5) the house church movement in China. In each case we shall discuss five major marks of revival movements:

1. Prayer always precedes a true revival: *prayer*
2. Revival is ignited when an anointed preacher or leader emerges: *leader*
3. New avenues of worship and music develop: *worship*
4. Revived believers seek to reach the least and the lost in society. This is sometimes called "Jesus living": *authenticity*
5. Revival permeates society with missional transformation. There is an intentional effort to shape society in a different mold: *missional transformation*

In order to build a full picture of past revival and reformation movements, we shall measure each by the same standard. Our standard will be the five marks of revival mentioned above.

Emerging Awakening—A Faith Quake

The Protestant Reformation

Prayer

Later in the history of revival we shall discover concentrated, well-defined prayer movements. However, during the time of the Reformation we must assume the existence of such pre-revival prayer. Martin Luther was drawn into a life of prayer by Catholic mystics. We find him reading the *German Theology*, a devotional approach to Christian truth. Even in his monastic life, Luther gravitated to devotional leaders such as Staupitz, vicar general of the Augustinian order. As a boy, Luther had come under the influence of the very pious Brethren of the Common Life. All of these influences converged to compel Luther to a devout, prayerful life.[1]

At the same time, Calvin came under reformational influence through a Bible study and prayer fellowship held in the Paris suburb of Meaux. There he met Jacques Lefevre, translator of the French Bible. Also in attendance was Margaret, sister of King Francis I. Through this devotional group Calvin became a strong believer and a man of prayer.

Leaders

Throughout the Reformation runs a golden cord of committed leadership. The most well-known name is Martin Luther, but he represents the tip of a large leadership iceberg. For instance, in the model city of Geneva, Switzerland the standout leader was John Calvin, a Frenchman driven from his homeland because of his reformational beliefs. In Scotland, the leader was an erstwhile galley slave, John Knox, whose preaching in Edinburgh ignited the revival. Hans Tausen served at the court of Frederick I and brought the Reformation to Denmark. Olavus Petri studied under Luther at the University of Wittenberg and he spread the Reformation to Sweden. Another Luther student was Michael Agricola, who birthed the Reformation to Finland.

---

1. Cairns, *Christianity Through the Centuries*, 288–89.

Worship

Prior to the Reformation, Christian worship had been defined narrowly by the canons of the Catholic Church. It was conducted solely in Latin, and music was likewise restricted to Latin. Congregational singing was unthinkable.

When Luther created the *German Mass* as a model for worship, he included congregational singing. The words were strong and reformational, as we see in his famous, "A Mighty Fortress is our God." He also penned the perennial Christmas favorite of all generations, "Away in a Manger." During the Reformation words were written in the vernacular and set to well-known folk tunes.

In Scotland, John Knox prescribed that the Psalms be set to music and sung in English, a practice that would dominate Puritanism. It even shaped the Anglican *Book of Common Prayer*, which was later bound together with *Hymns Ancient and Modern*. At any rate, congregational singing became the cornerstone of praise in post-Reformation times.

Authenticity

When we think of the Reformers, authenticity may not be the first characteristic that comes to mind. After all, most of them were fiery preachers and strong leaders. In reality they were also very honest in their quest for Christian living. For instance, in Geneva John Calvin taught the Bible every day. Common people flocked to hear him teach, and they found a warm welcome in the house of God. Luther produced a *Large and Small Catechism* so that children could be taught the truth of the gospel. Furthermore, the reformers had a strong social conscience. As war swept Europe, it was the Reformation believers who took in the orphans. Huldreich Zwingli, the Zurich reformer, died as a chaplain on the battlefields of the Thirty Years War. The roots of modern medical care are to be found within the ranks of early Reformation Christians.

Missional Transformation

Perhaps this is the most controversial aspect of the Reformation. Each of the reformers aimed to transform society. Most notable is the work of John Calvin in Geneva. There he set the city on a course of theocratic government. He sought to apply the ethical and moral standards of Christianity to society at large.

Luther cooperated with Prince Frederick of Saxony to shape a society within the framework of Christian principles. To this end, Luther created an established church, a church where all citizens of Saxony could belong. To be a Saxon was to be a Protestant. At the same time, to be a Bavarian was to be a Catholic. This intimate identification of religion and citizenship continued well into the twentieth century.[2]

In fact, the Reformation produced religious establishments throughout northern Europe. Each one was distinctive because of its ethnic connection. In Holland there was a strict Reformed Church. In England the Anglican Church was born from the royal will of Henry VIII. In Denmark, Sweden, and Finland the Lutherans were sanctioned by rulers. John Calvin was virtual ruler of the city of Geneva, as was Huldreich Zwingli in Zurich.

Only the Anabaptists challenged this concept of missional transformation. They created communal living situations where the church became the municipal community. Their descendants are found today among the Mennonite communities worldwide. A blot on their history was the perversion of this concept in Munster, Germany during the period of 1532–1534.

Pietism, Wesleyanism, and the Great Awakening

Prayer

The very word, "pietism," speaks of prayer. German pietism shaped the awakenings that swept Europe, the British Isles, and the New World during the eighteenth century. Aboard ship on his way to America as an unconverted missionary, John Wesley encountered a group of Moravians. Their prayerful calm amid a storm caused young Wesley to wonder. He craved the peace they displayed and would not give up his search until he found it in a Moravian meeting off Aldersgate Street, London. Wesley had returned in utter spiritual defeat, but the simple life of the Moravians and their reading of Luther's commentary on *Romans* turned the tide. Wesley recorded in his *Journal*: "I felt my heart strangely warmed. I felt I did trust in Christ, Christ alone, for salvation; and an assurance was given me that

---

2. Ibid., 296–97.

he had taken away my sins, even mine, and saved me from the law of sin and death."[3] The prayers of his Moravian friends wed to those of his godly mother, Susannah, had brought the new birth to Wesley.[4]

Leaders

The eighteenth century presented a remarkable array of revival leaders. In Europe it was the scholarly August Francke, who brought the ideas of pietism to reality. He had read Philip Spener's *Pious Desires*, and at the university city of Halle Francke introduced the intimate small group Bible study and prayer fellowship. He ignited a fire of revival that would sweep the western world. It is interesting to note that George Muller was converted in a Bible study near Halle. This occurred while Muller was a reluctant student at the University of Halle. Later he would house two thousand orphans in Bristol, England.

John Wesley also was caught up in the wave of awakening when he met the Moravians. They inculcated in him the ideas of lay-lead Bible study, which resulted in the Methodist class system. Every believer was engaged in a small group for purposes of spiritual growth.

Wesley's University of Oxford friend, George Whitefield, sailed to America, where he joined Jonathan Edwards to launch the Great Awakening. Seldom in the history of the Christian church has there been such a convergence of committed and godly leaders. Add to Whitefield and Edwards luminaries such as Gilbert Tennent and Theodore Frelinghuysen and one senses the depth of leadership for revival in the eighteenth century.

In many ways the eighteenth century awakenings created the concept of "evangelical" Christianity. In fact, British authors often refer to the work of Wesley as an evangelical awakening. The word, "evangelical," is derived from the Greek work for "good news," or gospel. It was the network of revival in the eighteenth century that recalled to collective memory the role of an itinerant evangelist, one who traveled far and wide preaching the gospel good news.

---

3. http://www.forthegospel.org/articles/the_conversion_of_john_wesley (accessed September 19, 2012).

4. Tucker, *Parade of Faith*, 378–89.

Emerging Awakening—A Faith Quake

Worship

New life brought with it new songs. German pietism spawned a prolific band of song writers. Likewise the Moravians added an entirely new hymnology, most of which was mystical and devotional. Charles Wesley wrote the ringing words, "O for a Thousand Tongues." It was this same Charles Wesley who shaped hymnology most of all. From his pen flowed an estimated 6,500 hymns. Many of them are still used: "Jesus Lover of My Soul," "Love Divine," and "Hark! The Herald Angels Sing," to name just a few. Actually, the Wesleys translated several German hymns into English and thus preserved the pietistic hymnology for the Christian church.

Notice that the Wesleys broke away from the singing of Psalms. They devised hymns that better expressed the spiritual experience of the worshipper. Worship is recast as a personal experience between the individual and God. It is significant because pietism, the Wesleys, and the Great Awakening all reintroduced the biblical concept of personal faith.

Authenticity

Within the revival movements of the eighteenth century there was also a renewed drive to demonstrate authentic Christian living. For instance, when Jonathan Edwards was expelled from his pastoral charge in Northampton, he took up residence in a mission house in Stockbridge, Massachusetts. There he sought to reach the Housatonic Indians, and his impact was not by preaching, but rather by authentic community living. His efforts were largely without success, and local historians have deleted this activity from memory.[5]

Not only did Jonathan Edwards reach out to Native Americans, but he also published the journal of David Brainerd. Brainerd had been engaged to Edwards's daughter, Jerusha, but the young man died before they could marry. To perpetuate a passion for reaching Native Americans, Jonathan Edwards published Brainerd's journal. It became a moving force in the modern missionary movement on both sides of the Atlantic.

In England, John Wesley spent his time with working class men and women. He had been barred from preaching in Anglican Churches because of his fiery sermons, so he initiated the practice of "field preaching." The Wesley monument at Hanham Mount, near Bristol, demonstrates this devotion. Each day at the end of a long, tedious workday hundreds of miners

---

5. Tucker, *Parade of Faith*, 393.

would ford the river to gather at a grassy hillside. There John Wesley daily preached the gospel of God's grace and mercy to them. Surrounding the town of Hanham are numerous large Methodist chapels, mute witnesses to the success of Wesley's dogged determination and authentic witness.

Missional Transformation

Not only did the revival preachers of the eighteenth century strive to reach people on the fringe of society, but they had a larger vision also. They sought to effect true social change. Perhaps the most loathsome practice of the eighteenth century in both England and America was slavery. It was at this point of deepest need that the revivalists tried to make their greatest impact.

In 1791 John Wesley was homebound. No longer could he ride out on his horse and preach in the open air. He sought to put his affairs in order as death drew near. First, he made provision for his beloved Methodist societies. These were clusters of committed Christians within the Anglican Church. The Methodist Church would not emerge until the nineteenth century.

Second, the dying patriarch addressed himself to the evil of slavery. In his last letter he wrote to a young member of parliament for Yorkshire: William Wilberforce. Wesley referred to slavery as "that execrable villainy, which is the scandal of religion, of England, and of human nature."[6] Then he charged young Wilberforce with a solemn task. Here are Wesley's exact words: "Unless God has raised you up for this very thing, you will be worn out by the opposition of men and devils. But if God be for you, who can be against you, who can be against you? . . . Go on, in the name of God and in the power of His might, till even American slavery (the vilest that ever saw the sun) shall vanish away before it."[7] In reality, this was John Wesley's last known letter, and it encouraged Wilberforce to take up the battle. By 1803 the slave trade in England had been abolished, and the evil institution of slavery was gone in 1833.

Finney, Moody, and European Awakenings

As Americans, we are somewhat familiar with the revival movements led by Charles Finney and Dwight Moody. These efforts were concentrated in

6. Hyde, *The Story of Methodism*, 237.
7. Loizides, "Church History Blog."

the latter half of the nineteenth century, but revival actually occurred off and on throughout the entire period. Recent scholarship has also turned up a network of revivals on the continent of Europe during the nineteenth century, the post-Napoleonic era. In an earlier work, I attempted to tie these divergent movements together.[8]

Prayer

It was the bloody French Revolution and the ensuing wars with Napoleon that drove Europe to its knees in prayer. One incident illustrates this. At a festive dinner celebrating the defeat of Napoleon at the battle of Grossbeeren, King Frederick William IV of Prussia spoke: "Who won the battle of Grossbeeren?" he asked. He bushed aside several answers and declared: "I will tell you who won. We did not, we only played a part. The man who won the battle is Pastor Jänicke [a Moravian], who spent day and night with his congregation kneeling and calling on the Lord, our God."[9]

The revival movement in Europe during the first half of the nineteenth century was seen to be the direct result of the "wars of liberation" from Napoleon. Christians prayed for victory, and they saw every triumph as a direct gift from God. When ultimate victory came at Waterloo in 1815 a revival movement was underway in many European countries.

Another remarkable prayer event occurred in New York City. Office workers found their way to the fish markets in Fulton Street for a noon prayer meeting. After 1857 this prayer revival swept across the United States following the simple pattern of Fulton Street. Ironically, no famous name was ever connected to this prayer event and ensuing awakening.

Leaders

Across Europe, Britain, and the United States there was remarkable diversity in leadership. Elizabeth Fry was one of the first Quaker women to be ordained. She took her dual ministry of prayer and prison reform to the palaces of Europe. In fact, the conversion of Prussian King Frederick William IV can be traced to her visit.

---

8. Detzler, "British and American Contributions," 2–7.
9. Ibid., 17–18.

In Scotland the Lord reached Robert Haldane. He later moved to Geneva, where he led a Bible study movement that issued in the French *Réveil*. In Germany the parallel awakening was led by Baron von Kottwitz in Berlin and the Krummacher family in Wuppertal, among others. While von Kottwitz was a lay leader, the Krummachers were pastors of the established church. John Michael Sailer led a renewal within the German Catholic Church. Sailer was a priest who later became a bishop. The diversity of leadership was equaled only by its depth.

In England the awakening centered on Cambridge, where Charles Simeon served as vicar of Holy Trinity Church. At the same time Henry Venn was vicar of Clapham Parish Church south of London.

Demonstrating the diversity of leadership, Timothy Dwight ignited the so-called Second Great Awakening in America. As grandson of Jonathan Edwards he had long been exposed to revival. He was installed as president of Yale University. From that vantage point he launched an awakening that swept the country east of the Mississippi River. Later in the awakening, Charles Grandison Finney traveled throughout New York and Ohio with his powerful brand of holiness preaching.

Worship

In the French-language movement, worship took a devotional turn. Several hymns were written by Cèsar Malan. Perhaps he is best known to modern worshippers for his song "Take My Life and Let It Be Consecrated Lord to Thee."

In many ways the most prolific hymn-writer of the nineteenth century was Fanny Crosby. This blind resident of Bridgeport, Connecticut produced hundreds of hymns and gospel songs. Among them are "Blessed Assurance," "Jesus, Keep Me Near the Cross," and "To God be the Glory."

It is no stretch of the imagination to say the nineteenth century marked the highpoint of modern hymnology. Many of these tunes survived long into the twentieth century. The famed *Moody and Sankey Hymnal* was used by evangelical believers in England until the end of the twentieth century, one hundred years after the death of Moody.

Emerging Awakening—A Faith Quake

Authenticity

From Germany, across Britain, and spanning the United States, the revivals of the nineteenth century were marked by a renewed emphasis on authentic Christian living. In Germany there emerged small fellowship groups (*Gemeinschaften*). Under humble, godly lay leadership these clusters of believers were scattered throughout Germany.

In America the awakening took an even more earthy twist with the emergence of camp meetings. Many of these revival events took place on the frontiers of Kentucky. At the Cane Ridge camp meeting in 1801 an estimated crowd of ten thousand came to enter into the atmosphere of exciting worship and compelling preaching of camp meetings. These led to the emergence of Bible conference grounds across the United States.

Missional Transformation

While the great battle of the nineteenth century was the abolition of slavery, Christians also took up many other causes. Ford K. Brown's noteworthy book, *Fathers of the Victorians*, demonstrates the breadth of concern among British believers. Among these battles were anti-slavery, prison reform, alcoholic recovery, and child labor reform.

The German immigrant George Muller blazed the trail in creating Christian orphanages. Even Charles Haddon Spurgeon started an orphanage in London. Pulpit power was often turned into a clarion cry for social reform. At Muller's home the administrator tells this story. Spurgeon had preached in Bristol and received about 600 dollars for his ministry. He planned to use it for his own orphanage, but his conscience caused him concern. So, on Monday morning he visited his dear friend George Muller and gave the money to him. When Spurgeon arrived back in London his mail contained more than 600 dollars for his orphanage. The amount of money is insignificant, but the passion for missional transformation is at the very center of revival in Europe, Britain, and America.

Pentecostals and Jesus People

Prayer

There is a rather loose connection between the Pentecostal revival of the early twentieth century and the Jesus People movement of the mid-century. However, for the sake of our study we will consider them together.

During the period of 1904–1916 a Pentecostal revival blazed in California, and it is named the Azusa Street Revival because of its point of origin. When the African-American evangelist William Seymour arrived, his teaching was rejected because he had not yet experienced baptism in the Spirit and speaking in tongues. However, he was invited to stay in the home of Edward S. Lee, where he launched regular Bible studies and prayer meetings.

Three days into an intended 10-day fast Edward Lee began to speak in tongues. Seymour immediately started preaching on Acts 2:4 and soon others also spoke in tongues. After an all-night prayer meeting Seymour himself finally spoke in tongues. This was hailed as a baptism in the Holy Spirit.[10]

Leaders

At the turn of the twentieth century Charles Parnham launched Bethel Bible College in Topeka, Kansas. One of his first students was William Seymour, who soon abandoned the college for an active ministry of evangelism. Seymour founded the Apostolic Faith Mission in Los Angeles. Here he pursued revival preaching, which ultimately became the basis of pentecostal theology. Most notable was the ethnic mixture among Seymour's flock: men, women, children, Black, White, Hispanic, Asian, rich, poor, illiterate, and educated.[11]

The Jesus movement, or "Jesus People," emerged during the late 1960s and early 1970s in California. It arose from the hippie culture, which was a counter-cultural movement. Actually, Duane Pederson named the movement in his *Hollywood Free Paper*. The name, "Jesus freak," was a pejorative

---

10. Tucker, *Parade of Faith*, 447–48. Cairns, *Christianity Through the Centuries*, 457–58.

11. Wikipedia, s.v. "Azusa Street Revival."

term applied to these zealous young Christians by the media, and often by more traditional Christians.[12]

Chuck Smith gave enduring expression to this movement with the founding of Calvary Chapel in Costa Mesa, California. Here he blended solid teaching of the whole Bible, book by book, with exciting, contemporary worship. This movement has spread across the North American continent and around the world under the vigilant and visionary oversight of Chuck Smith.[13]

Worship

Worship in the pentecostal revival at Azusa Street was marked by "singing in the Spirit." Often it was a free song sung in tongues, as worshippers simply gave vent to the movement of the Holy Spirit. The formal structure of hymns seemed too restrictive to them, and they experimented with new harmonies and words of ecstatic praise.

By comparison, the Jesus People adapted gospel beat music to their purposes. They played the same style of music but wrote Christian words for it. Out of the Jesus movement came a virtual galaxy of Christian musicians such as Barry McGuire, Second Chapter of Acts, Petra, Phil Keaggy, and Keith Green. When Paul Stookey came to faith in Christ he began to move away from Peter, Paul, and Mary, a dominant folk group. Paul Stookey became a leading light in the creation of worship music for the Jesus movement.

Chuck Smith founded the first Christian rock label when he launched Maranatha Music in 1971. This gave a commercial release to the new genre of worship music that was developing at Calvary Chapel in Costa Mesa and across the country. Pat Boone, another well-known rock-and-roll singer, founded One Way Records as a further commercial outlet for the music of Jesus People.

The Jesus movement heralded a break with traditional hymn-driven worship and the dawn of praise music. By the end of the twentieth century many churches worldwide have moved away from the historical "hymn sandwich," (hymn, prayer, hymn, offering, hymn, sermon, hymn, and benediction). The format for worship became more fluid with the majority of time being given to "worship," praise music, and less time to preaching.

---

12. "A Brief History of the Jesus Movement."
13. Calvary Chapel, "Our History."

Authenticity

Perhaps it was the Jesus movement that most exemplified the move to more authentic Christian living. The signal was visible. Instead of wearing dress clothes to church, worshippers showed up in casual clothing. It was not unusual in the early Jesus movement to find men and women wearing blue jeans and casual shoes, or no shoes at all.

When pressed for an explanation, the worshippers declared that they were stripping away all pretenses. This was a visible demonstration of authentic Christian living. As can be imagined, some traditional congregations were shocked. There were times when ushers turned away young Christians with no shoes on. It mirrored the ubiquitous signs in malls: "No shirts, no shoes, no service." Slowly, however, traditional Christians began to adapt to this visible authenticity. By the end of the twentieth century, even traditional churches had transitioned to business casual dress for Sunday worship. The concept of authenticity was marked forever on the face of Christianity across the world. Whether or not this authenticity marked the lifestyle of believers remained to be seen.

Missional Transformation

At first, the pentecostal movement was otherwise occupied. For much of the twentieth century, pentecostal Christians sought to define themselves and understand their own movement. However, by the middle of the century the Assemblies of God became a major force in missionary outreach.

When postwar Europe opened to American missionaries the Assemblies of God capitalized on the opportunity. They soon founded Bible colleges, especially in Belgium and Germany, and these became virulent centers of church planting. So much so that by the end of the twentieth century pentecostal Christianity was well-established on the European continent. The flourishing of Pentecostalism in Europe was aided by the work of Corrie Ten Boom and her spiritual allies, the Protestant Sisterhood of Mary in Darmstadt, Germany.

Even the Jesus People branched out in missional transformation. They expanded their outreach across the United States with large and thriving Calvary Chapels. These became springboards for missional outreach both in the United States and overseas. Perhaps it was the long life of Chuck Smith that gave both stability and strength to this vision.

At the same time, John Higgins began the Shiloh Youth Revival Centers. This offshoot of the Jesus People targeted college-age young people, as a majority of Americans attended college in the late twentieth century. By the end of the century, more than 100,000 young people were engaged in this missional movement.[14]

China's Hidden Christians

It is estimated that there are more than 80 million Christian believers in China. In fact, one government estimate put that number an estimated 67 million.[15] About 20 million are part of the Three-Self Patriotic Movement (TSPM), which is a religious movement controlled by the Communist government. In essence, it is a state church.

The remaining believers are part of the unregistered church, the house church movement. They meet secretly across the length and breadth of China. Usually they are housed in private homes, often apartments in the great cities and small villages of China. If there is an epicenter of this movement it might well be in the historical center of China, Henan and Hunan provinces as well as Beijing. And more than 80 percent of all house church leaders are women, according to a reliable source inside the house church movement. Certainly our experience has confirmed the truth of this allegation.

Across China there are more than one thousand underground training centers. Young people between the ages of eighteen and thirty are sent for prolonged periods of time to study the Bible. They are often taught by visiting instructors such as we are. Students arrive at the secluded centers carrying nothing but a small backpack. They live together with their teachers in a safe house, where intruding police or TSPM functionaries cannot find them. When the center is compromised it closes down as students and teachers move on to the next place.

With this brief introduction we turn to consider the house church movement as a modern-day revival. It has certainly revived Christianity in China. When Mao Zedong brought the revolution to China in 1949, there were scarcely one million Christians. In 1980 when China reopened to the

---

14. "Jesus Movement."

15. "Global Christianity." Some government statistic estimates there are up to 130 million believers in China. Perhaps this is a "scare tactic" to energize the Communist faithful.

West there were upwards of 50 million believers. That number has increased markedly since the 1980s. So, how does this revival look from inside?[16]

Prayer

It is widely assumed most join house churches because they have been healed. Stories of people being healed from diseases abound, and some even report having been raised from the dead. Attempts to verify these phenomena are predictably difficult. Nevertheless, prayer is very important in the house church movement. Each Sunday 40–50 believers gather in apartments or houses across China. Sometimes there are only a few believers, like one group we met in northern China. The Sunday service is full of energy. Usually the singing is spontaneous, and it is often accompanied by dancing. The teaching of Scripture is the centerpiece of the morning, and speakers often teach for more than an hour. In one center I taught an hour, and my wife taught for another hour after me.

After teaching, the floor is open for prayer. One by one worshippers come to the leader and kneel before him or her. The leader lays hands on each person and prays for specific needs, such as healing, deliverance from demonic power, or conversion to Christ. These prayer sessions can easily last up to two hours, and the church members surround the leader as he or she prays for the one in need.

A second aspect of prayer is even more dramatic. Very early in the morning students in each training center quietly get up. They have spent the night on a bamboo mat spread on a concrete floor. Quickly, they wash and ready themselves for prayer, and by 5 o'clock they are kneeling on the hard concrete floor crying out to God. In southern China especially they weep and wail as they pray. These simple Christians are known colloquially as "weepers." Prayer consumes at least an hour before a breakfast comprised of a bowl of rice and maybe a rice cake. The power of this prayer ministry is overwhelming, and I never tire of hearing my brothers and sisters cry out to God. Undoubtedly, the greatest honor of my life was the time spent in teaching the members of the Fengcheng church in Henan province.

---

16. Aikman. *Jesus in Beijing*, 5–18.

Leaders

The Fangcheng Church continues the work of Hudson Taylor, who served in this area during the second part of his missionary career. Leaders often visited us in central China, and they reminded us we were teaching in the church Hudson Taylor founded. He is regarded as the grandfather of the house church movement.[17]

Another patriarch of the movement is the late Wang Mingdao. Hudson Taylor's grandson, James Hudson Taylor III, said of Wang, "No Christian Chinese leader in the twentieth century has more clearly articulated the power of the Gospel of Jesus Christ, or more poignantly experienced what the Apostle Paul described as 'the fellowship of sharing in his sufferings.'"[18]

Wang and his wife, Debra, were jailed for more than twenty years because of their outspoken witness for the Lord. Wang Wingdao was imprisoned in 1958 and released in 1980, five years after his wife had been released.

Another leader of the house church movement is Allen Yuan. He too was imprisoned for more than twenty years because of his faithfulness to the cause. Billy Graham visited him during a trip to China in 1994. He explained to David Aikman that each year he held one baptismal service. At that event in 1998 he baptized a total of 316 new believers.[19]

These well-known leaders are a visible sign of a much larger host of heroes. Li was a young woman when I met her. She lived with us as our assistant and translator during the stays in China. One morning she began to tell of her imprisonments and beatings. Women were often hung by their thumbs, stripped of all clothing, and prodded with electric cattle goads. Still, Li never gave up. She persisted in traveling and preaching, even though it meant prolonged absences from her husband and dear little son. Informed sources tell me there are more than one million full-time itinerant workers in the house churches of China.

Worship

Worship is simple in the house churches. Whenever one asks, the road always leads back to one young woman: Xiao Min. She was born in rural Henan province and finished her education at middle school. Still, she has produced

---

17. Ibid., 74.
18. Ibid., 56.
19. Ibid., 59–60.

more than one thousand worship songs for the house churches. So dominant is her role that her songs are even sung in the Three-Self churches.

Xiao Min explains her remarkable ability in these simple words: "So often, during prayer time, quiet time or time of meditating on God's Word, the Holy Spirit would come and bring me a verse or two. Usually within five or ten minutes, I'll be singing the hymn with melody and lyrics."

The words are compelling and the melodies are haunting. I remember speaking at a conference of 40–50 young house church pastors in a remote village outside Beijing. Each morning they clustered to pray outside our window, and then the singing began. The words and tunes of those songs are engraved on my heart and will be until I die. This is true spiritual worship in every sense of the word. It reminds me of Paul's injunction to use, "psalms, hymns, and spiritual songs" (Col 3:16). Much of the singing is a cappella, which causes some to suggest that many Chinese have perfect pitch due to the tonal nature of their language.

Xiao Min is a young mother who commits herself to the creation of worship music for the house churches. She writes down the words in a simple tablet and sings the tunes into a hand held recording device.

Although authorities have tried to silence her by imprisoning her, she has enjoyed a merciful time of release during recent years. She believes God has kept her out of prison so the flow of songs will not be diminished. She is the heart of worship in the house church movement. Many of the details in this section are derived from Xiao Min's niece, who was a student in one of our training centers.

Authenticity

The word "authenticity" seems too small to embrace life in the house churches. Having met several dozen leaders across China, I have never noticed any sign of pretense or pride. Their only concern seems to be the safety of the church, the body of Christ. Most of the leaders have been imprisoned and tortured for the cause of Christ.

In fact, they seem to live a life of forgiveness. Li tells the story of a particularly brutal policeman who arrested and tortured her. As he poured out his venom and rained down abuse on her she prayed. Never did she betray her brothers and sisters in the church, nor did she beg for mercy. She simply prayed.

Emerging Awakening—A Faith Quake

Sometime later God answered her prayer. The aged father of that abusive police officer was converted. When the old man became a believer he commanded his son to stop persecuting the church. But this means the crusty cop was tamed. All of this came not through protests, but through prayer.

The first leader we ever met was a woman named Tau (not a real name). She worked as an evangelist for many years in Hebei Province. While jailed she was burnt all over her body with lit cigarettes, beaten, handcuffed and hung, and deprived of sleep for three days and nights. Her response: "This is to be expected . . . I prayed, 'God help me overcome this persecution. Enable me to continue to follow and love you. Don't only save me but make me an overcomer.'"[20] After several hours of reporting, Tau concluded with this ringing statement of authentic purpose: "We must overlook our persecution, give up our houses, endure beatings. When we feel the weakest our strength is in Jesus."

Missional Transformation

While living in central China we met many leaders of the dynamic Fangcheng movement. One of those who visited us was also a leader of the Back to Jerusalem movement. This is the overseas missionary outreach of the house church movement.

The explanation is simple: "You Western believers brought the Christian message to us. Now we are determined to take is back to Jerusalem." An elementary understanding of geography demonstrates the difficulty of this task. Between the borders of China and Jerusalem are the great Muslim powers of the world: Iran, Iraq, Syria, to name just a few.

Our students had already experienced this. Their summer internships took them to Egypt, where missionary activity is unsafe at best and deadly at worst. Others went into the hostile atmosphere of Myanmar, Burma. Still others served in Uzbekistan or Afghanistan. They came to us for missionary training, realizing they might well be called upon to give up their lives. When we asked the leader of Back to Jerusalem movement about this he responded frankly: "We are called to send our workers to the ends of the earth. We do not anticipate that they will ever return safely."

If their vision is geographically expansive, then it is personally astounding. The leader explained there are approximately one million full-time workers in the house church movement. It is the vision of Back to

20. Detzler, unpublished Diary, July 25, 2005.

Jerusalem that a tithe of 100,000 missionaries be sent into mission work throughout the Muslim world.[21]

Just as Renaissance era tradesmen traveled to Rome with silk, so missionaries wish to follow the same path. The Silk Road, as it is called, winded through Asia, Turkey, and Greece, until it reached Rome. It is this same route Back to Jerusalem workers will follow as they take the treasure of their living faith across the world.

Sister Anna led the house church in our town. She asked us to show a video of the Auca martyrdom in 1956. It is a cartoon version, but the message is strong. Throughout the showing Anna and Margaret, my wife, sat with their arms around each other. At the end Anna was in tears as she led our students into further commitment for missional transformation around the world.

Summary

From the Reformation to modern-day China, revival has characterized the Christian church over the past five hundred years. It is safe to say our five marks of revival are indicative, but not exhaustive. In a doctoral level course I taught on revival we considered several other characteristics. For instance, we discussed the renewal of biblical preaching as part of revival. Certainly this was the case during the Reformation, when for the first time in a thousand years the Bible became available in the vernacular language of the people. Luther led the way, and Calvin developed such preaching into a fine art. The same was true of John Wesley and George Whitefield.

Likewise, we could concentrate on the amazing numerical growth of the church during periods of revival. This is seen in the dormant America church under the Great Awakening preaching of Jonathan Edwards and his contemporaries. Dwight L. Moody's preaching created a thriving form of Christianity on the frontiers of the Midwest, and it thrived for almost one hundred years afterward.

Nor have we given due attention to the effects of revival on education. Many of the major theological institutions had their roots in revival. Princeton arose from the atmosphere of the Great Awakening, and Jonathan Edwards served as president at the end of his life. The Moody Bible Institute was founded by Dwight L. Moody and still exists today. Oberlin College

---

21. Aikman, *Jesus in Beijing*, 196–99.

had its roots in the work of Charles Grandison Finney. Surely, revival gave impetus for the establishment of many institutions for higher learning.

Nevertheless, we have settled on five characteristics of revival. Prayer seems to precede and power revival throughout history. Most great revivals are identified with the name of some leader, or many leaders. Worship forms are often shaped by revivals. Inevitably, revived believers deal with inconsistencies in their lives and a renewal of authentic Christian living ensues. Finally, both at home and abroad, missional transformation marks every major revival movement.

2

Core Values of the Emerging Church

THE CONCEPT OF CORE values is relatively recent. The government-sponsored National Leadership Council releases a fact sheet to demonstrate the value of developing core values. They are "those values we hold which form the foundation on which we perform work and conduct ourselves." Core values remain constant in an ever-changing world. They are not strategies for doing work, nor are they descriptors of the means used in doing our work. "They are the practices we use (or should be using) every day in everything we do."[1]

One note is necessary concerning the terms "emergent" and "emerging." Scot McKnight best summarizes the difference: "Emerging is the wider, informal, global, ecclesial (church-centered) focus of the movement, while Emergent is an official organization in the U.S. and the U.K. Emergent Village, the organization is directed by Tony Jones, a PhD student at Princeton Theological Seminary and a world traveler on behalf of all things both Emergent and emerging."[2]

The very presence of a governmental fact sheet indicates that core values are not always understood, nor are they appreciated. When I contacted a pastor at International Christian Fellowship in Zurich and asked about core values, it appeared to be a foreign concept. Annelies Strupler, a cofounder of the Fellowship, wrote: "[Our core values are] to see a relevant church for young people. The style of the services needs to be adjusted to that age group. The core value is to reach out to unchurched people,

---

1. National Leadership Council, "Core Values," http://www.nps.gov/training/us/whcv.htm (accessed February 2012).

2. McKnight, "Five Streams of the Emerging Church."

therefore the church needs to be value-driven."[3] A statement of mission is here substituted for a list of core values.

Josh Feay of Sanctuary in Fairfield, Connecticut spoke of a suspicion concerning core values in general. Feeling they are somewhat simplistic, Feay defaulted to the core values of the host church, Black Rock Congregational Church. He noted that a list of core values for Sanctuary had been developed, "but they never caught on." Josh Feay points up two major issues with core values. First, they must be meaningfully and repeatedly communicated. Second, they must be rooted in the essence of the organization.[4] Perhaps this is best summarized by Steve Furtick at Elevation Church in Charlotte, North Carolina. They have developed a code that places their core values front and center. It defines in great detail the behaviors expected of both pastors and attendees. To quote a spokesperson: "The Code is our core set of values at Elevation Church. It sets the tone and trajectory for how we get things done. If the mission is the compass, The Code is the map that gives us direction."[5]

Scot McKnight quotes Eddie Gibbs and Ryan Bolger in a list of nine core values common to many emerging churches: (1) They identify with the life of Jesus; (2) They seek transformation of the secular realm; (3) They live highly communal lives; (4) Because of these commitments they welcome strangers into their circle; (5) They serve with generosity; (6) They participate as producers; (7) They create because they are created beings; (8) They lead as a body; (9) They take active part in spiritual activities.[6]

Given the alienation of young adults from church in general and evangelicals in particular, it is imperative we get a grip on core values in emerging churches. Contact with lead pastors is powerful, because their commitment to core values is so clear, so complete.

It seems as if older generations have missed the point on core values, presuming this to be an artificial list of rules to be imposed on a church. In reality, core values are a description of the way any given church serves its generation for Christ. For this reason, it is crucial people buy into the core values of a church. Otherwise, they will never be at home in that fellowship. For instance, Justin Kendrick says it loud and often: "We exist at Frontline City Church to spread the lifestyle of authentic Christianity for the glory

3. Strupler, email to author, December 27, 2011.
4. Feay, email to author, December 27, 2011.
5. Villarreal, "Elevation Church."
6. McKnight, "Five Streams of the Emerging Church."

Core Values of the Emerging Church

of God and the transformation of society." This is the mission statement of Frontline Church, but it issues immediately in an authentic lifestyle shaped by the core values of the community. (In 2012 the name Frontline was removed, and the church became simply City Church.)

On January 1, 2012 Frontline hosted "Breakfast Church." When people arrived, a sumptuous breakfast meal was set out in the school cafeteria where the church meets. The chatter of children mixed with conversation around the tables. It was truly a family affair. At a given point Justin Kendrick stood, led a song, and cast a vision for the new year. It focused on developing community groups, and it revolved around the vision "to see actual change in the city of New Haven." Then Justin broke the group up into discussion clusters at each table.

At Transformation Church in Fort Mill, South Carolina NFL football-player-turned-pastor, Derwin Gray, is equally emphatic: "The Vision of Transformation Church is to be a multi-ethnic, multi-generational, mission-shaped community that loves God completely, ourselves correctly and our neighbors compassionately." The core values of Transformation Church derive from their mission statement, and they are carefully articulated on every possible occasion.

By surveying the core values of emerging churches, you can see how deep their commitment runs. Not all lead pastors march in lock step, but certain values seem to motivate life in many emerging churches.

Small is Big

In previous generations stretching back to the nineteenth century, churches have concentrated on numerical growth. In fact, during the mid-twentieth century Donald McGavran became professor of missions at Fuller Theological Seminary. He developed a formula for church growth, which issued in a church growth institute based at the seminary. This concept was rooted deeply in the American idea of a mega-church.

The Millennial or Mosaic generation values individualism, and this can best be cultivated in face-to-face relationships. Our hi-tech society has a strong hunger for hi-touch relationships.

Despite the explosive growth of Elevation Church in Charlotte, North Carolina, lead pastor Steve Furtick is committed to suitable size. He has multiple services in multiple locations, and none of them holds more than 500. This stands out in dramatic contrast to traditional evangelical and

Catholic churches. Many Charlotte churches seat two to four thousand. They foster worship as an event, while focusing on an authoritarian sermon. Furtick makes the point that this does not move Mosaics, Millennial generation believers.

In Bristol, England an emerging church is Bristol City Centre Church. Lead pastor Mark Detzler locates his worship in a modern, street-level hotel bar. It is open to passersby and attracts young adults who mill around the historic harbor side of Bristol. The bar would seat about one hundred. When they started a search for larger premises the church also considered intimate venues, where people can relate to each other. Before each service coffee and refreshments are served to promote community at Bristol City Centre Church.

When Justin Kendrick launched regular weekly worship at City Church he found a newly opened high school for the arts near Yale University campus. The centerpiece is a well-equipped theater that seats a maximum of three hundred. Kendrick is also committed to multiple services to keep an atmosphere of intimacy in the theater.

No matter how ambitious the outreach event is, emerging church leaders seem to sense the need of individuals. When City Church sponsored a citywide event on New Haven Green, 1,400 people registered. Immediately, Kendrick and his servant team focused on building relationships with individuals. Mass events are simply a vehicle to forge friendships. The real ministry is pursued on a one-to-one basis as members of the frontier team made contact with each of the individuals.

Mosaics get their information from a smart phone. They attend massive concerts if necessary, but they basically cluster with smaller groups. Community is much more important than colossal congregations.

Despite his distrust of the concept of core values, Josh Feay makes frequent reference to the need for small groups. Each Sunday the main meeting of Sanctuary is surrounded by an intimate prayer fellowship. Over the years this has been one of the main prayer centers for the entire church, and its influence is as intense as it is unheralded. Only when I have spoken at Sanctuary have I plumbed some of the depths of the prayer ministry. Community is a golden thread running through this key aspect of Sanctuary.

This emphasis on personal significance is buttressed by the spiritual dynamic of emerging churches. Dan Burrell at Life Fellowship in Huntersville, North Carolina was asked about the influences that shape this thriving ministry to Mosaics. One of the books cited is Watchman Nee's *Normal*

Christian Life. This one was forged in the furnace of suffering, and it reflects the intimacy of spirituality as seen throughout revival movements.

Grace at Work

Grace is more than a word. In the emerging church it colors everything they do. According to David Kinnaman, Mosaics mourn over the overprotective approach adopted by their parents, the Baby Boomers. They call this a "helicopter culture." Parents hover around young adults trying to keep them safe from every danger, conceivable or inconceivable.[7]

Traditional churches have also followed this pattern as seen in the restrictive sexual teaching of both Catholic and Protestant churches. A legalistic approach to sexual teaching has alienated many Mosaics. They want a reasoned approach to this and every other subject. For instance, Mark Driscoll's recent e-book, *Just for Men*, shocked both Baby Boomers and Elders. Mosaics found it helpful because it is honest.[8]

The frank nature of Driscoll's work reminds us of the need for discernment. As a new generation navigates through the maze of technological, cultural, and social changes, they need wisdom. It must be a high priority of the emerging churches to guide people toward true wisdom. Kinnaman urges a multi-generational approach to developing wisdom within community.[9] This is grace in action. Grace in the New Testament is often found in verb form, as a mode of action, not just a warm and fuzzy feeling.

Speaking from the context of southern Christianity, Derwin Gray echoes the same priority on grace. In summarizing the approach of Transformation Church to people in need, Gray asserts: "We are committed, through the Spirit's enabling power, to be a community that invites and seeks out the wounded, the broken-hearted, and the marginalized so that they can be transformed by the Gospel of grace into the image of Jesus joining Him in His mission to transform the world."[10] There is an inextricable link between community, grace, and wisdom-development in the emerging churches.

Scot McKnight calls this "praxis-orientation." The emerging church sees its end result as learning to live out the Christian faith. Rather than splitting hairs over doctrinal differences, the emerging church craves a

7. Kinnaman, *You Lost Me*, 96.
8. Driscoll, *Just for Men*.
9. Kinnaman, *You Lost Me*, 103.
10. Gray, email to author, October 5, 2011.

Emerging Awakening—A Faith Quake

reality-based faith. Orthopraxy is more important than orthodoxy.[11] Without deprecating the Millennial generation, one must notice this is part and parcel of postmodernism.

The deconstruction of doctrinal models is a significant development in the early twenty-first century. It forces biblical preachers within the emerging church movement to evaluate their methods and their message. For instance, Justin Kendrick has devoted a good deal of attention to the concept of substitutionary atonement, Jesus's atoning death on our behalf. Kendrick uses a broad array of telling illustrations, and he repeats the concept in almost every message. This reinforces the truth without creating a legalistic table of beliefs.

Yet another example is the recent e-book by Mark Driscoll. He challenged men in the Resurgent Movement, and his e-book soon went viral. It discussed sexual authenticity in blunt terms. Driscoll's purpose was plain. He wanted the young men in emerging churches to practice authenticity in their sex lives and marriages. This adds up to zero personal tolerance for pornography and promiscuity. Driscoll see this as a matter of God's grace in every area of our lives.

A theological note may be appropriate at this point. Mark Driscoll is committed to traditional Reformed theology in the mold of John Piper. It is well to remember that many of us older theologians speak of Reformed theology as "the doctrines of grace." What appears to be rigorous, restrictive lifestyle preaching is in reality a demonstration of the grace of God permeating every relationship in our lives. Thus we insist on calling it "the doctrines of grace."

Reclaiming the City

After World War II prosperity propelled American families out of the cities and into the suburbs. Incidentally, the concept of suburb was almost unknown until the 1950s. The cities were abandoned to minority groups who were often warehoused in sleazy tenements. Churches followed toe crowd and moved from city center to suburban garden greens. City center became a seething sociological cauldron of drugs, danger, and demoralization.

The merging churches have reversed that trend worldwide. Young people are moving back into the cities and claiming them for God. When Heinz and Annelies Strupler established the International Christian Fellowship

11. McKnight, *Five Streams*.

(ICF) in Zurich they re-claimed an old factory and turned into a state of the art worship center. The English name appealed to the new cosmopolitans, the Mosaics. Worship is loud, raucous and bilingual, English and German. Sermons are interpreted into various languages so that the multi-ethnic population of Zurich can enjoy it. Pastors are young and approachable.

Previous generations have fostered a fortress mentality for the church, but ICF broke that mold. By hiding out in their holy huddle many Christians have sought safety. In the process they have tried to insulate and isolate their young, protecting them from the secular society of the outside world. Frankly, Mosaics cannot wrap their minds around this exclusive, even excluding, approach to church. They want to see fairness and experience civic righteousness in their communities. To quote Justin Kendrick at City Church: "We want to see actual change in New Haven: businesses expanding, streets that are safer, and honesty in government."[12]

Heinz and Annelies Strupler projected this vision when they established International Christian Fellowship (ICF) in Zurich. Leading a young team of spiritual visionaries they took over a disused industrial site and converted it for worship purposes. It is nestled in the city center of Zurich, and each Sunday hundreds get a warm welcome as they come through the doors. It is a haven in the midst of a fast-paced culture.

When Mark and Cathy Detzler looked at the city center of Bristol, England they found the same picture. Ancient, Victorian churches stood empty as mute witnesses to a forgotten faith. Only a handful of them still had Sunday services. Others had been converted into stores, garages, even Hindu temples. As a result, Bristol City Centre Church set out to capture the heart of the city for God.

Breaking down the walls that keep Christians safe is never an easy job. The elder generation often misunderstands. They think the younger believers are seeking novelty for its own sake. In fact, the Anglican Church in England has been resolute in its decision to lock the doors of downtown churches to emerging ministry. To be fair, the same could be said in the United States. Here too abandoned churches often remain empty, rather than hosting new and vibrant ministry.

From a practical standpoint, Bristol City Centre Church even found problems when it tried to use an abandoned Anglican Church. The age-old building was constructed for formal, ritual worship. Attendees came for an hour each week and shivered in their coats against the winter chill. When

12. Kendrick, New Year Sermon, January 1, 2012.

Emerging Awakening—A Faith Quake

Bristol City Centre Church tried to adapt the building they discovered there were not even working toilets in the building. Case closed.

This forces emerging churches to seek creative solutions for worship. Justin Kendrick has twice taken Toad's Place in New Haven, Connecticut. Toad's Place is a rock music venue just a stone's throw from Yale campus. Every major group has appeared there. So the manager was willing to talk with Kendrick. On Easter, Kendrick launched his ministry to New Haven with an event at Toad's Place. Almost two hundred turned up for this first foray into the city center. When Christmas rolled around they again chose Toad's Place. This time more than 250 came to see the new show in town. As people entered the leadership team met them with a welcome and a try of goodies.

The evening flew by with Christmas music, dramatic presentation, even innovative graphic art. Kendrick tied it up with the Christmas message. Afterward, while the leadership team served Christmas cookies, others prayed with those who were seeking the Christ of Christmas. Like many of his contemporaries, Kendrick calls Jesus the Boss. His question is this: "Have you discovered that you are the lousy boss of your life? If so, you can invite Jesus tonight to become Boss."[13] This seems much closer to the Bible idea of Lord than anything I have ever heard.

This compassion for the city is found across the emerging church movement. In Charlotte, North Carolina it is Elevation Church that is best reaching into the heart of the Millennial community. When Steven Furtick first opened Elevation Church they met at a large high school in south Charlotte.

For two decades it had been assumed that south Charlotte was well-churched. After all, the biggest Catholic Parish welcomes thousands to mass each week. Major Protestant churches also line up along the southern axis of the city. So, as a careful observer and former pastor in a large church, I had wrongly assumed south Charlotte was reached. The explosive growth of Elevation since 1990 did cause me to wonder, however.

Pastor Furtick did more than wonder. He stepped out to start Elevation Church. In the Elevation Code it is straight up: "We need your seat. We will not cater to personal preference in our mission to reach this city. We are more concerned with the people we are trying to reach than the people we are trying to keep."[14] This is bold and even offensive to comfortable Christians, but it is the secret to revival in this generation.

---

13. Kendrick, Christmas sermon at Toad's Place, December 18, 2012.
14. Villarreal, email to author, October 12, 2011.

Core Values of the Emerging Church

The Code of Elevation concludes with this powerful phrase: "We will not take this for granted. What we are experiencing is not normal. This is the highest calling and we will remain grateful for God's hand of favor."[15] There is a heightened sense of purpose as they reach out to a city known for its churches. They realize the Mosaic generation has been bypassed by traditional Christianity, and Elevation is determined to reach them with the message of Jesus Christ.

Move from Charlotte to New York City and the atmosphere changes once again. "The Big Apple" is suave and sophisticated. Broadway brings the best singers, the best dancers, and the best actors every day of the week. From Times Square to fifty-seventh street is a center for television that informs and transforms public opinion around the nation and the world. So, how can a church reach New York City? How can this city be captured for God?

A generation ago it was Jim Cymbala who took up the challenge at Brooklyn Tabernacle; now there is a new generation and a new approach. It is Hillsong NYC. One Monday morning the leadership team summarized Hillsong NYC with this statement: "Last night at the *eXchange* was special. They're always special, but last night was *'specialer.'* That's right, so special we had to make up a new word for it. A beyond capacity crowd was in attendance for a night where our lead pastor Carl Lentz taught on the sacrament of communion. It was a moving experience for all—and a powerful, tangible reminder of one of the cornerstones of our faith."[16]

Notice the blend of historical Christian practices, such as communion, with the edgy approach to reaching metropolitan New York. We are reminded that this method is tried and tested. Hillsong began in New Zealand and spread to Australia. They also have a thriving outreach ministry in the United Kingdom. It is fascinating to note that Hillsong is one of the few ministries that has made the transition from Baby Boomer worship music to Mosaic or Millennial ministry. They have never lost their focus of reaching the city centers of the world with openhearted worship ministry.

One further illustration demonstrated the urban impact of the emerging church. This one is taken from Melbourne, Australia. Kevin Butterfield is one of the clearest thinkers and most persuasive leaders in the emerging revival. Kevin is an evangelist of city ministry. Since moving to Australia he has gathered around him a group of Christian leaders dubbed as "firestarters." They represent the Anglican Church in Australia as well as

---

15. Ibid.
16. Lynn, Hillsong NYC, email to author, November 2, 2012.

Baptist Churches. Kevin is lead pastor in a Vineyard fellowship. In Anglican churches Kevin hosts "New Wine" conferences, a reference to Jesus's promise that he would always bring new wine for each generation. Cities in Australia too are responding to the "new wine" of emerging revival.

Authentic Community

Each expression of the emerging church seems to be motivated by a quest for authenticity. At Elevation the core values explain it clearly: "We think inside the box. We will embrace our limitations. They will inspire our greatest creativity and innovation."[17] There is a refreshing absence of pretence in the worship experience at Elevation. It is loud and it is vibrant, but there is always a sense of authenticity about it. Put in the words of the Code: "We eat the fish and leave the bones. We will always maintain a posture of learning. We seek to learn from everyone and incorporate a variety of influences into our methodology."

On my first visit to Elevation we were hosted by one of the children's pastors. He had been a missionary kid in the church we served, and I had taught him during his freshman year at a nearby university. As we walked through the children's area there was a deep commitment to care for the kids and to nurture in them a sense of authenticity also.

Down the road from Elevation is Transformation, where the lead pastor is Derwin Gray. He summarizes the vision of Transformation Church in these words: "The vision of Transformation Church is to be a multi-ethnic, multi-generational, mission-shaped community that loves God completely, ourselves correctly, and our neighbors compassionately." Derwin Gray has committed his life to giving strong biblical leadership to other African-American pastors, and he and his wife live as brilliant examples of a biracial family. This gives solid and exciting meaning to authenticity.

Authenticity is the key word at City Church in New Haven. At Christmas Justin warned about the one-dimensional person, people who are "flattened out." From day one Justin Kendrick has emphasized authenticity. "Authentic is finding real in a culture of fake."[18] Every aspect of Frontline is shot through with a call for real life transformation. In his first Sunday at their permanent

---

17. Villarreal, email to author, October 12, 2011.
18. Kendrick, Christmas at Toad's Place sermon, December 18, 2011.

Core Values of the Emerging Church

home Kendrick said: "Now is the time for spiritual awakening to spread across New Haven County and for the resurgence of authentic Christianity."[19]

Three weeks later it was put to the test. Kendrick and two of his co-leaders stopped to help a driver who had run out of gas. It was midnight on a dark stretch of the scenic Merritt Parkway in Connecticut. As the driver coasted down the hill toward a gas station, Kendrick and his friend returned to their car. At that very moment, a speeding SUV crested the hill and slammed into the back of their car. Kendrick's executive pastor Miah (Jeremiah) was horribly injured. Immediately, the fellowship gathered at one of their homes and prayed through the night. What a demonstration this is of authentic Christian living.

The same sort of a story emerged from Bristol City Centre Church. A young family from the church had come to America on vacation, only to have one of their daughters hospitalized with a serious illness. Immediately, the church reached out across the ocean. The pastor and his family were also in America, and they interrupted their vacation to minister to their friends. A church near the hospital joined in to provide aid for the family. Authenticity knits believers together, when Christ followers pass through a period of need.

This new wave of authentic Christianity has caught some off balance. Peter Oborne recently wrote an article in the *Daily Telegraph* of London. His title said it all: "The Return to Religion." For instance, in 2004 David Stroud birthed Christ Church London, an emerging church within the Anglican community. "From a sociological point of view," says Stroud, "the attraction is a longing for community and a search for meaning. We preach an orthodox Christian message. Do that well and you have to lock to doors to keep them out."[20]

Kevin and Kerry Butterfield have taken authenticity to a new level in Melbourne, Australia. On one visit back to the States someone asked Kerry if she was an evangelical. Her answer was immediate and impassioned. "No," she said, "never call me an evangelical." Then she explained their passion for authenticity in the Christian life, something they had missed in traditional evangelical churches.

At the Vineyard in Melbourne their mantra is authenticity. There is no room for fakers here. Kevin calls this an era of "New Wine," when God brings new life into the sleepy shape of worship as usual. In fact, Butterfield

19. Ibid., sermon, September 18, 2011.
20. Oborne, "Return to Religion."

speaks at conferences that carry the name "New Wine." But this means he hopes to infuse authentic spiritual life with the existing structures of religion, even as he spreads the vision of new life.

Dan Burrell is not only the executive pastor of Life Fellowship in Huntersville, North Carolina, but he is also an astute analyst of the emerging revival. The mission statement of Life Fellowship is terse but powerful: "To pursue at all costs, the passionate, God-centered life."[21] After many years in ministry, Dan Burrell joined the pastoral staff at Life Fellowship. He brings to the task his experience as lead pastor of a more traditional evangelical church, and with this background he is able to shape an authentic atmosphere at Huntersville.

Authenticity is not only part of new church efforts, but it is also seen in some of the older emerging church ministries. For instance, Josh Feay sets this tone at Sanctuary in Fairfield, Connecticut. On the back of his business card, Josh has the following phrase: "Sanctuary is an authentic community, growing closer to God and making a difference in the world."

Close observance of Sanctuary is very helpful. Each summer they host a series of community nights at the home where we live. Each time I notice more diversity and more authenticity. The questions they ask are more basic, and the responses of the servant leaders are more direct, more relevant. Josh Feay's passion for authenticity is paying off in the Sanctuary context.

One final example illustrates the importance of authenticity. This one comes from International Christian Fellowship (ICF) in Zurich, Switzerland. Annelies Strupler together with her husband, Heinz, founded ICF. With the perspective of a lifelong commitment to authentic Christian living, Annelies writes: ICF exists as a "relevant church for younger people."[22]

Hansjörg Stadelmann summarizes the authenticity of ICF with four lead statements: ICF is about multiplication, as the love of Jesus jumps from person to person (the German is even more colorful). Second, ICF is about the supernatural, because everything is possible for God. Third, ICF is relevant to the city, because we love the people of Zurich. Finally, ICF is about connectivity, because we are strong when we are connected to one another.[23]

---

21. Burrell, email to author, November 8, 2011.
22. Strupler, email to author, December 27, 2011.
23. Stadelmann, email to author, December 27, 2011.

Missional Serving

The term "missional" sounds strange in the ears of Baby Boomers and Elders, but it is meaningful to Millennials. Previous generations have structured, even compartmentalized mission. They have used denominational or faith missionary sending agencies to span the seas. Servers were recruited as volunteers, and donations were sought from a variety of sources. For several generations the very term "missionary" conjured up exotic images of extremely dedicated people slogging through the jungle in shorts and pith helmets. For Mosaics, however, mission has a different look.

David Kinnaman explains it by pointing to survey results.[24] Many young Christ-followers concurred with the statement: "I am a Christian, but the institutional church is a difficult place for me to live out my faith." To them the church seems like an unreal atmosphere. It is a spiritual hot house that fosters a faith that cannot survive the real world. As a pastor I was amazed at a number of home-schooled children who ultimately either left the faith or fell into various addictions. When forced to face the real world, they found no faith could fit the task. This microcosm helps to explain the larger defection from the faith, especially from an evangelical faith.

Among the emerging churches there is a desire to find faith strong enough to stand up in this world. Derwin Gray put it this way: "We are committed, by the Spirit's enabling power, to develop a biblical, servant-based community, in which we serve each other through our grace-gifts as we serve in our spheres of influence by being the heart, hands, and feet of Jesus."[25]

Serving is very practical for the emerging church. On a hot summer day, City Church took over the New Haven Green, a park in the center of the university city. They asked people to register their attendance, so that they could keep in touch. More than 1,400 signed in that day. Kids jumped on huge bouncing toys, while adults rode a mechanical bull. Serving members of the City Church community wore black T-shirts sporting the phrase: "I love New Haven."

True to their word, the team turned this into a serving opportunity. They donated 1,400 hours of service across the city, one hour for each attendee. City Church folks are sticklers for authenticity, and they always keep their word. From day one this core of committed Christ followers has gotten their hands dirty serving the folks in New Haven, Connecticut.

---

24. Kinnaman, *You Lost Me*, 79.
25. Gray, email to author, October 5, 2011.

Emerging Awakening—A Faith Quake

On New Years day City Church hosted breakfast church. It was a delicious meal served around a casual, very interactive worship experience. Several days later my cell phone rang. It was one of the staff from Frontier phoning to pray with me. He asked about what was going on in our lives and then passionately prayed. This is a whole new face for missions. It is missional transformation.

Now when they preach the good news about Jesus their message is credible. Today people are less concerned about preaching. They are more eager to see practice. Orthopraxy always trumps orthodoxy in the emerging church, as Scot McKnight has reminded us. Orthopraxy is identified by a smudged face and dirty hands.[26]

Hansjörg Stadelmann calls this missional transformation "city-relevance" (in German, *Stadtrelevant*). He explains this relevance with a terse phrase, "because we love the people."[27] Missional transformation is not about numbers. It is all about the people in today's cities. Annelies Strupler adds that ICF Zurich is committed to multiplying similar centers in every major city in Europe.[28] Already three similar fellowships exist in Switzerland, and each one is committed to multiplication.

Life Fellowship in Huntersville, North Carolina is more traditional in its doctrinal basis. In fact, Dan Burrell has come to the ministry after other pastorates in traditional evangelical, even fundamental, churches. He frames this missional approach in a generic way, "reaching out to God's world in a 'gospel' way."[29] No doubt Life Fellowship has had a strong impact on the northern suburbs of Charlotte, North Carolina.

Often lead pastors of emerging churches experience disconnect with more traditional churches. This is not theological. It is usually more methodological. A prime example of this is the work of Josh Feay at Sanctuary. Sanctuary was birthed at a traditional evangelical church in Fairfield, Connecticut. Under Josh Feay's leadership it has been developing its own character and imprint. Josh claims, "Mission is the reason we exist."[30] This is an intriguing statement, because the mother church is known for its million-dollar annual faith promise to missions. Josh seems to have a different idea, however. For him mission is all about showing compassion for the poor

---

26. McKnight, "Five Streams of the Emerging Church."
27. Stadelmann, email to author, December 27, 2011.
28. Strupler, email to author, December 27, 2011.
29. Burrell, email to author, November 8, 2011.
30. Feay, email to author, December 27, 2011.

and oppressed. Constantly, he stretches the Sanctuary attendees to make their faith relevant, to move from orthodoxy to orthopraxy. Although the mother church has a large footprint in overseas missionary work, Josh Feay also tries to direct the attention of Sanctuary folks to the practical challenge of living out faith where we are. Close to the affluence of Fairfield is the dire need of Bridgeport, and Sanctuary has been faithful in reaching out to that community. Much of this is due to the leadership of Josh Feay.

Elevation Church has fully integrated missional transformation into its lifestyle, and this colors all that happens in its various sites. The mission statement is short and simple: "So that people far from God will be filled with life in Christ." This mission statement is the compass and the code is the roadmap. Throughout the Code are key phrases that illuminate missional transformation. They speak of giving sacrificially to reach the city of Charlotte. Again they assert that the first priority is to reach the city with the message of Christ. Steven Furtick is passionate about sharing, even inculcating the mission in those who attend Elevation.

One example may illustrate this. When we visited Elevation we were directed to a guest parking spot, the best one in the lot. Before we got out of our car someone was there to greet us, and they walked us into the entryway of a converted mall super store. It seemed as if we passed through a colonnade of welcoming people. When the doors opened for the evening, we were ushered into front row seats and everything we would need for the evening was given to us. On the way out there were more welcome tents, and each attendee was given a black Elevation T-shirt. This over-the-top welcome is a very practical example of missional transformation. It sets apart Elevation from any other church in the church-rich city of Charlotte, North Carolina.

Missional transformation looks very different from either home or foreign missions in days gone by. Today's believers are not so concerned that their church or their denomination gets the credit. Missional to them means doing what Jesus would do in the down and dirty world of twenty-first century life.

Jesus Living

The phrase "Jesus living" may sound simplistic or shallow, but it is just the opposite. This is the main aspect of authenticity, as young adults wrestle with the complex issues of living out the life of Christ in a pluralistic and

Emerging Awakening—A Faith Quake

secular society. In their introductory handout, City Church makes it very clear: "We believe that God awakens cities. We aim to play a part in His plan to bring spiritual awakening to our city, our region, and our nation in the hopes of reaching the world with the gospel."[31]

Derwin Gray voices the idea differently, but his passion shows when he writes: "We are committed, through the Spirit's enabling power, to the belief that Grace is *Jesus Himself coming to live in and through His people. Life in the Kingdom is empowered by the King of Kings, not human effort* [italics mine]."[32] Although Derwin Gray's words sound formal, the idea is there. Transformation Church seeks to incarnate Christ for a new generation, children of the new millennium.

So central is this Jesus-living that Scot McKnight called one of his books *The Jesus Creed*.[33] There is a reverberating echo through the emerging church. It is this striving for the simplicity that characterized the Jesus People of a previous generation. Gibbs and Bolger bring a cautionary note, however. They remind us that the Jesus People were unable to jump the chasm they saw between the secular and sacred worlds. This led them to withdraw from the outside world and lose their potential impact on their contemporaries. By contrast, the emerging churches are passionately committed to bridging the gap between sacred and secular.

An example comes from the gritty post-industrial city of Waterbury, Connecticut. A young dental practice manager spotted a man on the street looking for lunch. Without thinking the high-drive executive bought a homeless man a meal. This commitment to immediate involvement is part of the DNA of the emerging church. Gladly they work outside the box to meet needs when and as they find them. This is a prime example of *missional* thinking versus out-of-date *missionary* thinking. Structure always comes second to serving in the emerging church.

As Justin Kendrick puts it: "Discipleship is a not passion to just follow Jesus. True discipleship is a passion to be like Jesus."[34] Like many emerging church pastors, Kendrick is committed to authentically living out the life of Jesus in a contemporary context. For this reason he is consumed with study of the gospel records. The concept of "the word becoming flesh" as found in John 1:14 is determinative. To quote Gibbs and Bolger: "As Jesus did, we

---

31. City Church, "Ministry Government and Structure." Unpublished factsheet. 2012.
32. Gray, email to author, October 5, 2011.
33. McKnight, *Jesus Creed*.
34. Kendrick, sermon, February 19, 2012.

must provide a critique, but that evaluation must come from within rather than be imposed from outside the cultural context."[35]

Previous generations have sought to contextualize the gospel message, but the Mosaics truly enculturate the message. Contextualization sometimes adapts the content of the message to make it more palatable to the culture, as Rudolf Bultmann snipped out the miracles to make the gospels more acceptable to a scientific, rationalistic German society. The emerging church tries to enculturate the message, to make it visible and alive within the culture of Mosaic young people. By living transparent lives they attempt to imbed the gospel message within their own culture. I have the impression this is indeed biblical community. For instance, City Church hosted a block party as one of their early events. Several of the families live in close proximity to each other, and they host the single members who need accommodation in the city. So, these neighbors threw a big block party. As I scanned the street scene there were believers everywhere touching and serving their neighbors, living out the life of Christ on the streets of New Haven, Connecticut.

In Peter Oborne's *Daily Telegraph* piece he cites Bishop James Jones of Liverpool: "'People have become more sensitive to the Christian faith.... When the material world gets knocked people are forced to think again, and that's when Christianity does have something important to say.'" Then the bishop concludes with this ringing endorsement of new church movements: "'People are aware there's a big shift in society coming along, even though they might not understand it. So I'm not surprised that the ground is now more fertile for the spread of the Christian message.'"[36]

It is not surprising that even traditional church structures, such as the Anglican Church, realize the need for a fresh approach to the Millennial generation. To their credit, they have also enabled creative young pastors to launch appropriate churches in the emerging church mold. I would hope these fresh new leaders will have the liberty to persist in their passion to reach a new generation. According to the *Daily Telegraph* piece, this has spurred a spike in church attendance, which usually catches the eye of the ecclesiastical powers that be.

Another aspect of Jesus-living is the way in which emerging churches use their resources. Do be blunt: Do they put their money where their mouth is? Derwin Gray claims that they do: "We are committed, by the

---

35. Gibbs and Bolger, *Emerging Churches*, 16.
36. Oborne, "The Return to Religion."

Spirit's enabling power, to financial generosity. We cannot out give our God; therefore, we will teach and live biblical financial stewardship. One day we hope to give away thirty percent of our income."[37] Remember Gray is an former NFL football player, who has known the high-rolling lifestyle of professional sports. This makes his commitment to the corporate generosity of Transformation Church even more intriguing.

Elevation Church embraces Jesus-living as the moving force in its worship. As stated in the code: "Simplicity enables excellence." We place a disproportionate value on creating a worship experience that boldly celebrates Jesus and attracts people far from God." Added to this is their commitment to generosity: "Our staff (pastors) and church will go above and beyond to give sacrificially to the work of God in our city."[38]

I sense among the pastors of emerging churches a refreshing desire to lead by example. They are not the "fat cats" we have seen in a generation of television superstars. These are men and women who lay their lives and their possessions on the line to live out Jesus's life before their faith communities. As an older pastor, I derive great joy and encouragement from the life and dedication of these emerging church leaders.

Dan Burrell summarizes this Jesus-living in the core values of Life Fellowship. One of them is, "investing in growth, chasing daily after the heart of God to become more like Christ." This one spills over into a commitment for "embracing our mission, reaching out to God's world in a 'gospel' kind of way."[39]

Gone is the fortress mentality. No longer are believers inside and unbelievers outside. There is no room in the emerging church for the "holy huddle." This new breed of believers is busy living out the Jesus life among their friends and neighbors. Lines of distinction are not drawn by taboo. They are sketched in the loving contours of Jesus's life. This is missional living at its very best.

All-Out Worship

In previous models there has been a sense of distance. Rather uncomfortable Boomers learned to raise their hands and clap awkwardly. Elder believers preferred to sit in reserved reverence and let worship music flow over

---

37. Gray, email to author, October 5, 2011.
38. Villarreal, email to author, October 12, 2011.
39. Burrell, email to author, November 8, 2011.

Core Values of the Emerging Church

them. None of this resonates with Mosaics. Although chapter 3 is dedicated to the practice of worship in the emerging church, I do want to mention the contribution of enthusiastic singing in this context.

Worship for them is all-out and all-in. No restraints color their worship, whether it is dancing to the music, raising what the Bible calls "holy hands," or singing at the top of their lungs. Derwin Gray caught the flavor when he wrote: "Biblically, we believe the essence of worship is Romans 12:1–8. We are 'living sacrifices' in worship. We call this worship a lifestyle." So worship is more than a song set to kick off Sunday morning, it is attitude of life. Then Gray added: "Worship through music at our weekend services is Christological. We want to spread the fame of Jesus. Stylistically, because we are a multi-ethnic, multi-generational church our music genres are diverse."[40]

Scot McKnight notices that worship is much more participative in emerging churches. Some describe this as funky worship, candles and incense, or smells and bells. From my standpoint, however, this trivializes what is happening. I sense that Mosaic worshippers want total, personal involvement. The spectator mentality of worship is fading fast, almost gone. This is true even when worship leaders are high-powered people such as Justin Kendrick and Zenzo Matoga, an exciting African worship leader (see chapter 3, "Vertical Worship"). The purpose according to Kendrick is "to see the Millennial generation moved by the gospel."[41] And they are moved.

Josh Feay explains that worship at Sanctuary is designed to help people connect with God in a way that enables and empowers them to live for God in their world. Worship music helps people reorient themselves back to a true focus on God. The entire atmosphere is designed for focus. Lights are dimmed to avoid distraction. Music is loud to drown out human influences.

Kevin Butterfield has grasped the significance of signs and wonders in worship. When he led Sanctuary in Fairfield, Connecticut, he often joined in worship leadership. Sometimes he played drums, and other times he actively led worship. Kevin knows how to set the tome and prepare worshippers to meet God in the moment of miracle. Healing and deliverance are twin manifestations of true spiritual worship for Kevin. This ultimately led him to his role as leader of a Vineyard Church in Melbourne, Australia.

Even in staid old England worship is changing. The infusion of life comes form Africa. Huge Pentecostal churches are springing up in the suburbs around Britain's cities, and they are alive with worshippers from

---

40. Gray, email to author, October 5, 2011.
41. City Church, "Ministry Government and Structure." Unpublished factsheet, 2012.

African countries such as Ghana and Nigeria. Often one church will host as many as ten thousand. Recently, the Redeemed Church of God reportedly drew a crowd of forty thousand to London's ExCel Center for an all-night session of prayer and worship.

Sometimes you must read between the lines to understand what emerging churches are saying about worship. Life Fellowship in Huntersville, North Carolina has deep roots in traditional American evangelicalism. The lead pastor, Bobby Conway, is a graduate of Dallas Theological Seminary. So, when Dan Burrell reports on worship, we must understand what he is saying. The purpose of worship at Life Fellowship, according to Burrell is, "to glorify the Lord through God-centered, Biblically-saturated, and response oriented worship that allows us to experience an awareness of the presence of God in our lives individually and corporately."[42] Notice again the emphasis falls on "vertical worship," focus on God and his power in our lives.

Elevation Church is primarily outward looking. They try to welcome true seekers and show them the way to Jesus. It even affected their form of worship, as they claim: worship is designed to "engage lost people, allow worship to happen among believers, and do it all with excellence."[43]

Mark Driscoll addressed this when he spoke to a Resurgence event in Orlando, Florida. "We must wait for the Spirit," he asserted. "We need to be filled like Jesus." For Driscoll, worship is all about the presence of the Holy Spirit moving through the meeting. He cites as one of the key elements of his Resurgence movement, "Spirit-filled life and theology." It is this Spirit-filled theology that leads us away from modernistic theology, such as some of the aberrations that have appeared among emerging churches.[44]

One more aspect of Mosaic worship breaks the mold. Both Baby Boomers and the Elders are very time-conscious. Worship for them should fit into a sixty-minute package. Half the time may be singing, but the second half must be preaching. In the Millennial community, time seems to stand still. After forty-five minutes of worship, the sermon may be equally as long. There is abundant time left for prayer ministry to all comers.

---

42. Burrell, email to author, November 8, 2011.
43. Villarreal, email to author, October 12, 2011.
44. Driscoll, "Four Points."

Marks of Emerging Revival

As we survey the core commitments of the emerging church, a pattern of revival begins to emerge. I seem to discern at least five characteristics of revival in the emerging churches.

Prayer of a Dedicated Minority

In Switzerland all-night prayer times awed and amaze us. It seems as if time stood still while they cry out to God. Notice the phrase, "cry out to God." It marked the early emerging churches in Switzerland. When we moved on directly from Switzerland to China there were more lessons to learn about prayer. One of the emerging churches in China has the nickname, "The Weepers," as mentioned in an earlier chapter. As they cry out to God they soon begin to weep. Living with these young believers, we were amazed that they slept on hard, concrete floors. At five o'clock they woke up seemingly without any alarm clock. Then there followed a solid hour of prayer, as they knelt on the same concrete floors.

Even in America this prayer power is evident. Five years before founding City Church Justin and Krissy Kendrick built their prayer team as priority number one. For five solid years they prayed for core members of the team. Nothing deterred them. They kept on praying, and the prayer team became the foundation of the new church. Before he preached the first time, Justin prayed with his team. He realized any true revival must be born of prayer by a dedicated minority.

Leader Committed Completely to God

Revival is almost always ignited by a single person sold out to God. This is as old as Dwight L. Moody. In Bristol, England a man knocked on his door and said this to Moody: "The world has never seen what could be done with a man sold out completely to God." Moody's ready response was this: "By God's grace I shall be that man."[45] The end result was a significant revival movement that swept America and Britain.

This experience rings true for the emerging churches. When you speak with Justin Kendrick, there is a sense that he is completely sold out to God.

---

45. http://desiringlife.wordpress.com/2007/01/27/the-world-has-yet-to-see-what-god-can-do-with-and/ (accessed September 20, 2012).

Emerging Awakening—A Faith Quake

As he puts it: "Being is bigger than doing. I want to be God's man before I try to do God's work." Scot McKnight finds this to be widely true: "One of the streams flowing into the emerging lake is prophetic rhetoric. The emerging movement is consciously and deliberately provocative. Emerging Christians believe the church needs to change, and they are beginning to live as if that change had already occurred."[46] When asked what leaders have shaped his ministry Kendrick responds: John Wesley, Charles Haddon Spurgeon, and Reinhold Bonnke. He also draws inspiration from Brian Houston of Hillsong Church in Sydney, Australia.

New Avenues of Worship

Perhaps the best example is the dominance of Hillsong. They have revitalized pentecostal thinking and this is fueling new life in many emerging church churches. It is especially conducive to the ripening revival movement.

Before he left New England Kevin Butterfield spoke with me. He had moved from an historical Anabaptist church life to a new openness to the pentecostal movement. When asked about signs and wonders, Butterfield explained how he expected healings and deliverance from evil spirits. In many ways, this triggered his emigration to Melbourne, where he could become an active player in the pentecostal movement. His leadership has been crucial in the revival movement among emerging believers in Australia.

Derwin Gray started his ministry in a Baby Boomer church within the Presbyterian community of faith. Soon he found discomfort in their attachment to forms. This catapulted him into the founding of Transformation Church at Fort Mill, South Carolina. There he has led a movement of revival among Millennial Christ followers.

In nearby Charlotte Steven Furtick pioneered the work of Elevation Church. His background is ironclad Southern Baptist, but he knew the need for a more suitable Millennial church. So, he broke the mold and opened Elevation Church in a large high school. Soon they had expanded to many different sites, each served by a campus pastor. Like a franchise business these sites adhere strictly to the Elevation model, and the revival among young North Carolinians goes on.

---

46. McKnight, "Five Streams of the Emerging Church."

Core Values of the Emerging Church

Reaching the Least and Lost in Society

Here we find the missional aspect of the emerging movement. Scot McKnight notes that they see this as participating with God in redemptive work within our society. Mosaics also seek to immerse themselves in the community where redemptive work is happening. It is a holistic groaning, learned from the picture of the Holy Spirit groaning for us in prayer (Rom 8:25–6).[47]

This passion for involvement has taken Justin Kendrick and his core group beyond the call of duty. Individual families have purchased large, old homes in New Haven. Their unabashed goal is to reach their community with the saving life of Christ. Their end goal is nothing less than transformation of the city.

Kevin Butterfield reports that young adults, mostly under thirty, are clustering together in the Melbourne area. Their aim is simple: to infect their community with the saving life of Jesus. They call themselves, "firestarters," because their stated purpose is to fan the flame of revival.

Attending Elevation Church reinforces this picture. The doors open minutes before the "service" begins. Young people quietly but firmly push their way into the small, dimly lit theater-style room. As you scan the crowd there are kids from every stratum of society waiting to meet God in the ministry of Steven Furtick together with his high-energy worship team.

At IFC in Zurich the look is different, more European. The room is full of clean-cut Swiss kids. Well-dressed, but casually-dressed Swiss young people crowd through the doors every time they are open. When the music starts, all reserve is gone. Worship is as enthusiastic as Boston Night of Worship or Hillsong New York. When they worship, the reserved Swiss shell cracks wide open. It is after worship that connection comes to life. All over, emerging churches kids cluster to talk to each other and to God. Some are healed and others are led to saving faith. The emerging church in some of its manifestations has the appearance of a revival, such as those I have experienced around the world.

Key to this dynamic atmosphere is a committed leader. Sometimes they are thoroughly trained theologically, such as Steven Furtick. He is a graduate of the venerable Southern Baptist Seminary in Louisville, Kentucky. Kevin Butterfield was trained at Alliance Theological Seminary, the Christian and Missionary Alliance school in Nyack, New York. Both Mark and Cathy

---

47. McKnight. "Five Streams of the Emerging Church."

Detzler studied at an Anglican Seminary in Bristol, England. Other leaders have learned through association as Justin Kendrick did. What unites all of these leaders is their commitment to transformation within society.

Revival Leads to Missional Transformation

Every conversation with Justin Kendrick comes around to New Haven. He is resolved to see a resurgence of biblical Christianity in the university city. He sees models in both Jonathan Edwards and his grandson, Timothy Dwight. Both of them connected revival to the Yale community.

Kevin Butterfield senses revival is already afoot in Melbourne, Australia. Each correspondence with him carries new reports of renewal and awakening. From the Vineyard Church in Melbourne there flows a flaming river of renewal throughout the entire country of Australia.

Derwin Gray emerged from the formal church life of Charlotte, North Carolina. New he expresses his purpose in these words: We are committed, by the Spirit's enabling power, to value people for more than what they can produce. "We will not prostitute people over and against their spiritual health and transformation."[48]

Already I see signs of spiritual awakening throughout the emerging churches. This seems to be a "first fruit" of things to come. Amazingly, many of the more theologically divergent leaders seem to be fading away. The thoroughly committed young leaders are going from strength to strength. This encourages me to pursue the prospect of an "emerging awakening—a faith quake."

---

48. Gray, email to author, October 5, 2011.

3

Vertical Worship—God Centered

WORSHIP IS OFTEN SHAPED more by culture than Scripture. Each new awakening brings with it a distinctive twist on worship music, and revival becomes relevant to every generation. This goes all the way back to the Renaissance. For centuries the Catholic Church had worshipped through chants, monotone repetitions of worship truths. Then came Giovanni Pierluigi da Palestrina. He served as organist in a Roman church and ended up in 1551 as leader of the choir in the cathedral of St. Peter. Here he lit up the worship with exciting, harmonic (polyphonic) music. Could it be that Palestrina's popularity is the Catholic answer to the Reformation emphasis on congregational singing?

It is no mistake Palestrina overlapped with the Reformation era. Martin Luther had revolutionized worship by introducing and popularizing congregational singing. This Germanic twist to worship stood out in bold contrast to all that went before. The words were solid statements of Reformation teaching. This is seen in "A Mighty Fortress is Our God." He also framed several Christmas hymns from "Away in a Manger" to a popular German song, "*vom Himmel hoch*" translated as "Give heed my heart, lift up thy eyes. Who is it in yonder manger lies?"

Luther tried to touch the emotions of the congregation in all of his hymns, and many have survived to this day. Truly congregational singing and worship can be said to be a product of the German Reformation during the sixteenth century. Many think Luther picked his tunes from the popular drinking songs of the day. This disturbs some purists, but group singing is based on familiarity with the words and the tunes. The more "singable" the tunes are, the stronger impact they have on worship.

Emerging Awakening—A Faith Quake

After the Reformation the Catholic Church sought renewal in what is known as the counter-Reformation. At the same time, Protestantism gained a distinctive worship pattern in the seventeenth century, known to European historians as the period of orthodoxy. Worship music is the brightest light during this time. Johann Sebastian Bach pens popular worship songs. Perhaps the best-known example of these is "Jesus, Joy of Man's Desiring."

I saw this popularity firsthand while preaching in a beautiful Lutheran Church near Lubeck, Germany. We recall that Bach lived at Lubeck. Our preaching mission lasted one week, and each evening the worship leader sang one Bach song prior to the sermon. It was particularly selected to fit the theme of the evening. To my utter amazement the congregation joined in and sang along wholeheartedly with each Bach piece. Congregational singing seems to have flourished during the Bach era.

In the eighteenth century England was the focus of revival under the leadership of John Wesley and his brother, Charles, who authored thousands of hymns. Remember also that John Newton, the converted slave ship captain, was a contemporary of Wesley. He has left us with one of the most popular worship songs of all time: "Amazing Grace." I believe this explosion of congregational worship in England was directly related to the revival atmosphere surrounding the Wesleys.

If we move on to the nineteenth century, America becomes the center of worship music. The traveling companion and worship leader for Dwight L. Moody was Ira Sankey. He wrote haunting melodies and penetrating words, as can be seen in a hymn like, "Under His Wings" and "A Shelter in the Time of Storm." He put the story of the lost sheep to music in a song, "The Ninety and Nine." Sankey published a revival song- book that served English congregations until the late twentieth century. These were revival songs calculated to inspire Christians and set them singing.

A fascinating bridge to twentieth century revival music was the blind hymn writer, Fanny Crosby from Bridgeport, Connecticut. She paved the way for "gospel songs," music that expressed the deep longings of the worshippers. For instance, she wrote, "Blesses Assurance, Jesus is Mine." This became a theme song for Billy Graham crusades until very late in the twentieth century.

Music always seems to express revival, and nowhere is this truer than the largely unreported revival that swept the cities of Chicago and Detroit in the first half of the twentieth century. Its musical roots ran back to Fanny Crosby and her collaborator, William Howard Doane. Although he was

Vertical Worship—God Centered

an independently wealthy industrialist, Doane's passion was always gospel music. He composed several hymns, and he also endowed Christian education in many places, such as Moody Bible Institute.

Moody was key to the spread of gospel music through an early Christian radio station, WMBI from the Moody Bible Institute. Here many Christian musicians were employed and the sound of revival music blanketed the greater Chicago area from the early 1920s onward. This impact was largely due to the station manager, Wendell Loveless, who himself authored many popular Christian songs. These gospel songs set experiential, heartwarming words to the swing rhythms and harmonies of the big band era.

During the middle of the twentieth century things began to change. The Baby Boomer generation had little or no connection to the revival movement of the early twentieth century. Their musical roots were deep in the genre of rock and roll, especially the music of the Beatles and Elvis Presley. Rock relied on a "rock solid" beat, a steady pounding rhythm that moves the song and the singer.

Out of the Baby Boomer generation came contemporary Christian music. It started with worship songs, such as "He is Lord" and "His Name is Wonderful." Some turned toward pure, God-centered worship music. By the end of the last century worship had become synonymous with music. To sing was to worship. Soft rock reached both young and old, but the Jesus People of California craved a stronger beat, and contemporary music moved from west to east across the United States.

At the same time groups like Hillsong United reached out from Australia to pioneer an exciting version of worship music. The arrival of Hillsong music in America was timely, because it coincided with the wave of contemporary worship in evangelical churches. Although the beat is ever-present it lacks the edge Mosaic young people need. They want music that is as real as it is really loud. Millennial kids want to feel lost in the sound and beat they can feel pounding in their chests. They approach this with the same vigor they bring to every other aspect of their lives. In some ways this is simply a characteristic of young adults in general, but Mosaic or Millennial worship cannot be explained solely as a generational matter. It is more than a music fad. It is a mark of true awakening and revival.

Millennials are moving away from the experiential music of the Baby Boomers. For instance, Baby Boomers sing about their worship experience, "We have come to say that you're our God." The emphasis falls on personal experience of worship and is deeply connected to the experience-centered worship of gospel songs. In most churches this is known as contemporary worship. Through this mode of worship many Baby Boomers have grown strong and deep in their own worship experience, they have learned to worship God with true abandonment.

However, the Mosaic kids want more. They want all-enveloping worship. In many cases they are asking for more "vertical worship," songs that focus on the glory of God alone and eclipse personal experience. We shall survey this vertical worship by a series of case studies, individuals, bands, and groups that have a passion for worship.

The Goal of Worship

The first question for worship leaders is this: "What is your main goal in leading worship?" On the surface there is diversity among worship leaders, but beneath the surface there is a deep unity.

Rebecca Refvik not only leads worship at Black Rock Church in Fairfield, Connecticut, but she has also trained and discipled many leaders from the Millennial generation. When asked about the goal of worship, she responded that the aim is to be a lead worshipper. Then she added: My goal is "to receive the love of God and to lavish God with our loving responses to his love. To portray an understanding of our beauty before God, blemishes and all."[1]

From the exciting experience of Elevation Church we receive a fresh approach. Chris Brown is worship pastor, and he explains that Elevation is primarily evangelistic, trying to reach unbelievers. So the primary of purpose becomes a demonstration of true worship. He explains: "We never get too 'churchy' or 'insider' with our language from the stage as we lead, so that the lost will not feel completely disconnected. But at the same time, we are going to passionately and unapologetically worship God and lead the people to do the same.[2]

Zenzo Matoga comes from Malawi, and he sees himself as a worship missionary to New England. His main ministry is the Boston Night of Worship. Additionally, he serves as worship leader at Jubilee Christian Church in Boston. When pressed about his goal for worship, Zenzo replies: "People gather from across culture, denominations, and social lines in desperation for God!" It is this passionate pursuit of God that powers worship for

---

1. Refvik, email to author, January 24, 2012.
2. Brown, email to author, January 26, 2012.

Zenso. He claims as a personal mission statement: "A burning passion to see the nations of the earth experience God in a tangible way."

A slightly different slant marks the worship ministry at Sandals Church in Riverside, California. Matt Richey serves in the worship ministry and he sees worship as our "musical offering to God . . . and it should be our best."[3] Sandals Church has a laser-like focus on authenticity. Their vision statement demonstrates this: "Real with self, real with God, and others." They expand it with the following core values: "Real with self—working towards where God has called me to be in Christ. Real with God—developing a relationship with God that produces spiritual fruit. Real with others—joining God on mission as a loving member of a local church."

From the standpoint of Sanctuary, it is interesting to compare the views of various leaders. Josh Feay is lead pastor of Sanctuary, and he sees the overall goal of helping people to connect with God. He discerns the goal of worship music as, "opening ourselves up to receive peace and joy from God's Spirit."[4] When I interviewed John Mendez, Sanctuary's worship leader, he explained further the purpose of worship. According to John, the purpose is to "glorify God. This is the main goal and must always be the thing that is first and foremost." From a personal standpoint he added, "As I worship God, I can enable others to do it also."[5] In a spirit of honesty and spiritual integrity, John Mendez warned: "My purpose is not to create a warm and fuzzy feeling." Worship for him is not about emotion, but rather about exposing the worshippers to a life-changing experience with God.

Mendez was cautious when he drew a comparison. He remarked that worship at Willow Creek Community Church is geared to the Baby Boomers. It is designed to make maximum emotional impact, to create an emotional response. At Sanctuary John strives to draw worshippers into the presence of God. The focus is not the performance of the band, but rather the focus on God and his presence in the worship center.

Derwin Gray sets the tone for worship when he says: "Worship through music at our weekend services is Christological. We want to spread the fame of Jesus." His executive director of worship ministries is Angela Lear, and she shared in depth the Transformation Church flavor of worship.

---

3. www.sandalschurch.com (accessed January 2012).
4. Feay, email to author, December 27, 2011.
5. Mendez, interview, January 20, 2012.

Emerging Awakening—A Faith Quake

According to Angela her goal is "to lead and engage others by personal example as we focus on praising a holy and magnificent God through music."[6]

Notice each of the worship leaders phrases the answer differently. They are divergent in both their skills and their approach. However, the underlying purpose is singular. It is to glorify God. Worship is like age-old stained glass windows. It filters the light and allows people to see God's glory, but it never obstructs or overshadows the glory of the living God. It is his glory alone that drives worship.

It was Mark Detzler who introduced me to the term vertical worship. He chooses worship songs that focus solely on the greatness and glory of God. Worship is not about our emotion, what Mendez calls the "warm and fuzzy feeling." It is exclusively an expression of worship and praise for God.

Justin Kendrick was lead singer of a band called Out of Hiding before he became lead pastor of City Church. Now he is both lead singer and lead pastor, and the band members are the heart and soul serving the church. They pray with people and counsel them after every service. Each time they rock through a worship set it reverberates with "vertical music," worship with God as the audience of one.

The same God-centered worship warms hearts in Zurich at International Christian Fellowship. Both worship and those who worship exemplify the multi-ethnic flavor of ICF. It is as if the church is a microcosm of the cosmopolitan city of Zurich. Singing blends German, Swiss-German, English, French, and indeed all the languages that make up a throbbing, Millennial meeting. Preaching is in Swiss-German with high quality simultaneous translation into other languages.

Annelies Strupler and her husband founded ICF. They keep close contact with the exciting outreach of ICF. Annelies adds about the worship: "The style of services needs to be adjusted to the age group (of Mosaic or Millennials). . . . The worship is modern with many of their own songs. It's their style of music. It is the style of today's society. Of course, the message is clear, biblically based. But it is adapted to today's life."[7]

In order to broaden our base of information I interviewed Erika Khamarji, who has several years of experience in leading worship. She summarized her goal as serving God—the focus is on God alone. Then she added explanatory information. "It is glorifying him through words and music for

---

6. Lear, email to author, January 24, 2012.
7. Strupler, email to author, December 27, 2011.

all that he has done and is doing in my life. It is also about leading others, whether they are believers or not, in what worshipping God looks like."[8]

To summarize the goal of worship, despite the diverse approach and geographical situation of various worship leaders, the goal seems to be the same. It is to glorify God and to reorient the view of worshippers to they will focus completely on God and his glory. I sense single-mindedness among Millennial worship leaders. They believe warm and fuzzy emotion is too shallow. They will settle for nothing less than the glory of God.

It reminds me of a worship leader who changed my life. His name was Stuart Hine, and he wrote the hymn, "How Great Thou Art." As a pastor I was blessed to spend a couple of hours with him while he was suffering from cancer. Throughout our time together he emphasized and re-emphasized to me the overwhelming goal of giving God glory. Our Millennial friends have certainly gained a new grip on this priority.

Prayer Precedes Worship

Worship teams typically pray prior to worship. So I asked each leader, "What do you pray before leading worship?" A key to understanding worship is the prayer of worship leaders. Across the board I have noticed intensity about prayer among these very passionate people. They seem to get a grip on God better than most of us can. So I asked this question: "When you pray before the service what is your dominant drive?"

Elevation's Chris Brown explains that prayer has several emphases prior to the service. We come to God with hearts full of gratitude for what he has done in our lives and in our church. We also pray with the expectation that God will show himself to be real and present during our worship. We allow God absolute freedom to do whatever he wants to in our lives and in our worship. Personally, I have seldom if ever seen such spontaneity in worship as I experienced at Elevation.

Erika Khamarji has grown up in an atmosphere of worship, and she summarized her prayer passion with these words: "Praying before the service is . . . asking God to remove all distractions so that we can fully focus on what the Holy Spirit wants to do through us."[9] Then she added: Prayer is to "ask the Holy Spirit to be present in worship so that other may be touched." I notice among Millennial worship leaders a strong focus on oth-

8. Khamarji, email to author, January 20, 2012.
9. Ibid.

ers. This lifts it away from the performance mentality that always threatens a worship experience.

Josh Feay sets the tone for Sanctuary. He believes "Sanctuary is an authentic community growing closer to God and making a difference in the world."[10] The God-ward emphasis shapes worship at this Fairfield center. Josh has brought John Mendez into the worship ministry at Sanctuary, and Mendez thinks very deeply indeed about the process and purpose of worship.

When I asked John about his prayer priorities, he responded thoughtfully: His point of departure is a deep awareness of need, and he focuses on connecting the worshipper with God. This will enable God to move in their lives in a more authentic way. Authenticity permeates all that emerging churches do, and this is especially true of the ministry at Sanctuary.

John made the point that he wishes to avoid pretense in his clothing. He wears jeans and a T-shirt to lead worship. At first I thought this might be sort of a Millennial uniform. In reality, it is an effort to blur distinctions between people, to put everyone on level ground before Christ's cross.

"I pray that whatever happens it will be God at work," Mendez insists. Then he adds that the ultimate aim is the free movement of God's grace. In the midst of leading worship John prays that God will change lives, that he will have unrestricted access to the minds and hearts of worshippers. For Mendez it is not about a warm, fuzzy feeling. Worship revolves around a passion for the powerful presence of God.

When I asked Rebecca about prayer and worship leadership, she responded strongly. The two focuses of prayer are God's promises and the people's needs. Also, bringing the worship team together in prayer reminds them of why they are leading. They pray for their hearts, minds, and voices to be right, and they declare their dependency on God alone. Each week they cry out to God for a new anointing. She summarized: "We try to get the focus off us and on Jesus alone."

Rebecca included a powerful quotation from Charles Haddon Spurgeon in her response: "Prayer gives a channel to the pent-up sorrows of the soul, they flow away, and in their stead streams of sacred delight pour into the heart. At the same time the more rejoicing the more praying; when the heart is in a quiet condition, and full of the joy of the Lord, then also will it be sure to draw nigh unto the Lord in worship."

Another strong source of information about worship is Angela Lear. She coordinates creative arts at Transformation Church in Fort Mill,

---

10. Feay, email to author, December 27, 2011.

Vertical Worship—God Centered

South Carolina. When quizzed about her prayer priorities, Angela responded: "By the Holy Spirit's enabling power may our gifts and abilities be used for your glory and your fame. Let every action and each word point people towards you."[11]

Total dependence on the Lord characterizes true worship, and this is evident in several illustrations. During the Azusa Street revival in 1906 people sang a cappella, without accompanying instruments. There were extended periods of silence. There was prayer in tongues for the healing of the sick and for overseas missionaries. Soon people were mailing in prayer requests to the revival community in California.

A heart cry for God to intervene that drives much of the prayer in such revival movements. Prayer breaks free from formality. All over the room people are pleading with God to touch them, as they receive the fullness of the Holy Spirit. This is not only true in traditional pentecostal circles. I have also experienced it in the academic atmosphere of college awakenings. Even in staid, formal English Christianity I have heard people cry out to God for a fresh touch as the Holy Spirit moved through congregations.

Justin Kendrick underlines the potency of prayer with this statement: "We are hard-wired to hear from God."[12] A recent experience underlines the practical power of prayer for God's people. Together with the band Justin was returning on an old tour bus with the team of Holy Fire Ministries. As they drove through a desolate part of New York State an acrid odor became stronger. Holy fire took on a very dramatic meaning for the band as smoke curled from the rear engine compartment. Without taking time to collect their belongings, the band clambered off the bus and stood aside to size up the situation. Smoke turned to flame. At first small flames came from the engine compartment, and then they became bigger. The band called 911, but it took a long time for help to arrive. Prayer was more appropriate than a 911 call that day.

In the meantime they stood by helpless, watching all of their possessions go up in smoke. When a fire engine finally arrived it was too late. The bus had burned to the wheels. Nothing was left. Their clothing as well as their instruments were all gone. A friend came to pick them up and took them home. Once out of harms way they began to tabulate the losses. Clothing was all gone, as were their expensive instruments. Sadly they added up the losses, and the total came to 36,000 dollars. Still Justin and the team

---

11. Lear, email to author, January 24, 2012.
12. Kendrick, sermon, January 22, 2012.

know that they were "hard-wired to hear from God." So they cried out to him for a solution to their desperate need. Within a six-week period more than 90,000 dollars was given to the ministry, and the band was able to take up its itinerary again.

Prayer in the emerging church is marked by a refreshing dependence on the Holy Spirit to work as promised. Mark Driscoll underlined this in a teaching session before the Resurgence Movement. His title is: "Four Points of the Movement." He takes his listeners beyond historical Reformed theology and reminds them that God is the point of departure for all that do. Here again is that refreshing dependence God. Driscoll reminds us that the Trinity is not composed of the Father, the Son, and the Holy Scripture. It is rather the Father, the Son, and the Holy Spirit. He states boldly that cessationism is worldliness. In other words, people who believe the gifts of the Spirit have ceased are really bound by the rationalism of the Enlightenment age.

Then Driscoll reminds his hearers that there were miracles in the early church. As the Holy Spirit came upon Jesus at his baptism, so the Holy Spirit now empowers believers. Driscoll boldly asserts: "We need to be filled like Jesus was."[13] Perhaps this explains to some degree the refreshing dependence on the Holy Spirit we encounter in the emerging movement.

Again, we recall how this fresh approach to the ministry of the Holy Spirit fuels a renewed reliance on prayer. Worship in the emerging church is not simply a preliminary to the sermon. It is far more than that. It is an opportunity for people to meet God in a new and real way. This divine encounter is the substance of prayer by worship teams, and they are hard-wired to hear form God. They know that God will answer their prayer.

Influencers for Worship

Justin Kendrick set the tone with this powerful word: "Our praise supersedes our circumstances." With this challenge he launched worship at City Church on a cold Connecticut winter morning. It helped jump-start the worship process, and it lifted us all into the presence of the King.

In order to grasp the life of leaders, I asked them: "What other worship leaders have influenced you most?" Whenever I quiz worship leaders, one name seems to come up: Brian Houston. He is the founder of Hillsong, the formative worship ministry from Australia. Brian Houston belongs to the Baby Boomer generation, having been born in 1954 in Auckland, New

13. Driscoll, "Four Points of Movement."

Vertical Worship—God Centered

Zealand. At age 32 he moved to Sydney, Australia and gave birth to Hillsong as part of the Assemblies of God in Australia. Hillsong Church exploded in size until 20,000 were attending each weekend. Some of the favorite songs to emerge from this ministry are "Shout to the Lord," and "Might to Save." Now Brian heads Hillsong International Leadership College, as a training center for ministry. Hillsong TV network is also hosted by Brian Houston.

But the person of Brian is overshadowed by the powerful influence he has exerted on worship across the world. When I asked Justin Kendrick about his models in ministry, Brian Houston was high on the list. Brian Houston has further extended his influence through his team. A former worship pastor at Hillsong Church is Darlene Zschech.

Chris Brown adds the concept of mentoring to this discussion. He refers to Lee McDerment at NewSpring Church. During Chris's time at Anderson College (in Indiana) McDerment invested heavily in equipping Chris for worship ministry. NewSpring has experienced explosive growth among Mosaic worshippers. So, the role of Lee McDerment was particularly helpful in preparing Christ to lead worship at Elevation, which has experienced the same sort of expansion.

Angela Lear cites Darlene as one of her major influences. When Rebecca Refvik responded, she too mentioned Darlene Zschech as a source of inspiration. Darlene started out as a session singer producing TV commercials for Australia. She released her first album, an old vinyl platter, in 1988 under the title, "Pearls & Gold." One of her major contributions to the field of worship has been her writing. She has produced four books on worship: *Worship* (1996), *Extravagant Worship* (2002), *The Kiss of Heaven* (2003), and *The Great Generational Transition* (2009).

Although Darlene Zschech has worked strongly among the Baby Boomers, she has also set a model for Mosaics or Millennials. Her influence on the emerging movement has come through the young leaders she has touched. Now Darlene and her husband, Mark, co-pastor a thriving Hope Unlimited Church in New South Wales. They have also extended their outreach to Rwanda. It is interesting to remember that Rwanda and neighboring Uganda have been centers for a thriving revival movement ever since the 1930s. It seems as if this is a key place for Zschechs to make their impact in Africa.

Another name that crops up when I ask about influencers in worship is Chris Tomlin. He was born in 1972 and is part of the bridge generation between Baby Boomers and Millennials. He started his ministry at Austin

Stone Community Church in Texas. He is a major worship leader across the United States, especially at Passion events.

Chris Tomlin has blended old hymns with modern beat. For instance he took the traditional "Amazing Grace" and enhanced it by adding the refrain, "my chains are gone." He penned the classic worship staple, "How Great is Our God." Tomlin began his music-writing career at age 14. In the mid-1990s he became worship leader for the Dawson McAllister Youth Conferences. This catapulted him into the forefront of worship among the Mosaic generation. For this reason many worship leaders draw their inspiration from Tomlin.

An exciting new voice in the United States is Joel Timothy Houston. Joel is the son of Brian Houston, and recently Joel has come to New York City to establish Hillsong Church. Joel paid his dues by playing bass guitar in several bands. He was the bassist for Able, which swept the Channel V Leg Up competition in 2001. Then he joined his family in leading worship across Australia, South America, Africa, and Europe. More recently Joel joined Carl Lentz in launching Hillsong NYC, their exciting new worship center in New York. Even in suave, sophisticated New York, crowds snake around the block waiting for the doors to open at Hillsong. They have truly impacted the heart of the city with the worship of Hillsong.

One name emerged in my investigation that amazed me. It is Ron Kenoly, and Angela Lear cites him as a formative influence on her worship style. Ron is definitely a Baby Boomer, born in 1944 in Coffeyville, Kansas. His worship style marries exciting, jubilant praise with incredible musical skill, especially on the piano. Once I observed Ron Kenoly as he visited a large, fairly traditional church in Charlotte, North Carolina. He played stunning music on the piano, and then he moved to the gigantic pipe organ, one of the biggest in the United States. His musical skills lit the organ with worship. Ron is a musician *par excellence*. So, how can he be an influence on Millennial worship?

Ron spent several years in the United States Air Force, and afterwards he earned several degrees including a doctorate in worship leading. He was part of a group called Shades of Difference. He burst on the Christian music stage in 1992 with an album called *Lift Him Up*. Another album, *Welcome Home*, became *Billboard's* "top indie contemporary Christian music album."

His ministry was based initially at Jubilee Christian Center in San Jose, California. There he built a solid reputation in leading worship. He now speaks and leads worship around the country from his base in Florida.

His ministry has been expanded to some degree by his participation with the Inspirational Network (INSP) out of Fort Mill, South Carolina.

When People Respond

My next question to worship leaders is this: "How do you know when people are responding to your ministry?" Is it their enthusiasm and the loudness of their singing, or is there some other criteria that help you gauge response? This is perhaps the most difficult aspect of our section concerning worship. Angela Lear admits that this is difficult, perhaps impossible to assess. The most apparent answer is that the worship leader seeks participation. Sometimes the crowd is more responsive, and this can depend on many different, variable factors. Perhaps they are weary, or perhaps they have just come from the busyness of a workday.

Then Angela adds several criteria about the selection of worship songs:

- They must be chosen prayerfully.
- Songs must also be theologically sound, true to the teaching of the Bible.
- They must make much of God, by lifting him up.
- Also they must support the message being preached.
- Relevance in the genre of songs is likewise important.
- As is diversity in the genre of the songs, not monotonously the same.

Then it is up to the worship leaders to set the tone. They must sing to God, "as if it their last time on earth to do so."[14] Then the atmosphere of worship is electric, full of energy.

My mind flashes back to central China. Each Sunday we worshipped and taught in a house church, a group of about fifty believers clustered in an upscale apartment near the city center. Immediately, the believers mixed prayer and singing, but they soon asked us to teach them. After I had taught for about an hour, we took a pause in the proceedings. The folks had sat still for the entire hour on little, short, wooden stools. So, they now stood and began to sing.

As they sang the worship leaders began to sway, and soon the entire group was gently swaying and dancing to the music. There were no instruments, because security was of top priority, and instruments might attract

14. Lear, email to author, January 24, 2012.

attention. Only the pure, straight tone of human voices filled the room. It seemed as if this worshipful dancing and singing went on for about twenty minutes, and then the leader turned to Margaret, my wife, and asked her to teach for another hour. Seldom in my life have I experienced such a heartfelt response to worship.

My faith community background is diverse because of the various places we have lived and ministered. Having grown up in the gospel song era, it took some time for me to grow into present worship forms. Ironically, it was China that broke the mold and opened my heart and mind to new forms of worship.

Chris Brown is remarkably brief in his description of response to worship. His worship leadership is sensitive to what is happening in the crowd. "People get excited about Jesus," he notices, but also people are hurting and come for healing through worship. Some people look lost, and this motivates Christ in his efforts to connect with them.

Some of the same genuine worship characterizes Sunday at City Church in New Haven, Connecticut. Although he does not always lead worship, the lead pastor Justin Kendrick introduces it. "We magnify you, O God, through a heart that exalts you." He sets the tone before a very professional worship team takes over. Soon the whole crowd is on their feet singing, "You are glorious. You are holy." They intersperse this with the phrase, "Knowing that your grace brought us to this place." Bridging to various songs is singing in the Spirit, that pentecostal blessing that combines free harmonies with expressions of praise and worship. Not only is there almost universal involvement in worship, but time seems to stand still as the worship team leads us into the very presence of the Lord. At City Church even the amazing guitar and drum work seems to feed the energy of worship. Soon you forget the musicians and sense they are ministering to the Lord and drawing us into an encounter with eternity. To quote Justin Kendrick again, "Our praise supersedes our circumstances."[15]

When we turn to Sanctuary, we are reminded that this Millennial ministry is housed in a fairly traditional church—Black Rock Congregational Church in Fairfield, Connecticut. It was born out of the church, when Kevin Butterfield birthed it several years ago. Originally it was more like the contemporary worship of the Baby Boomer generation, but it has left that milieu behind.   Now Sanctuary is structured to reach and minister to the Mosaic generation. This becomes clear when we speak with the worship

15. Kendrick, City Church service, January 22, 2012.

leader, John Mendez. He too has put together a highly professional band, and he gives serious thought to the worship atmosphere.

The darkened room enables worshippers to concentrate on God and not on those next to them. The loud drum and guitar music makes it possible for everyone to sing along, having lost the inhibition of fear about being heard. Ironically, this has been a characteristic of revival movements around the world. I remember non-musicians singing loudly when I was a child, because they knew that no one could hear them. The same was also true of house church worship in China.

"What about physical manifestations of worship?" I asked John Mendez. He mentioned raised hands, but he added that other manifestations of worship also occur. Some people dance quietly, others bow face down to the floor as they worship. Many just stand with closed eyes to exclude the atmosphere and focus their worship on the Lord. There is definitely more physical worship at Sanctuary than was ever seen in the more traditional and contemporary worship experiences at Black Rock.

From a West Coast perspective, Sandals Church has its own worship response. Matt Richey is one of the worship leaders, and he applies the watchword of authenticity to the music ministry. He explains this goal is, "seeing where God takes us as we explore what it means to be real in our music."[16] Although this sounds somewhat cryptic, it communicates well with the student and Mosaic population who are building a great worship community at Sandals.

Rebecca Refvik is thoughtful as she assesses her role. She recognizes that people come to worship from various backgrounds, and they also bring baggage from the outside world with them. Some seem resistant to follow worship leadership, and perhaps this is a reflection of the burdens they bring to the task. Basically, Rebecca notices that the vast majority of worshippers connect each week with God. In many ways it breaks down the barrier erected by the busy life of Fairfield, Connecticut.

From her own standpoint, Rebecca speaks of the worship leader's attitude as a guideline for the worshipping community. She speaks of exhibiting exemplary devotion in the very process of leading worship. She sees the worship team as spiritual shepherds leading people into the very presence of God, and she concludes, "God is always growing our ability as

---

16. www.sandalschurch.com (accessed January 2012).

lleaders to communicate and radiate compassion and vulnerability toward the congregation."[17]

Erika Khamarji is representative of the Mosaic community when she describes her expectations during the leading of worship. First, she looks for the obvious and more usual signs that people are connecting with the living God. Some are raising their hands and singing their hearts out, while others are reticent. Then she adds: "It is awesome to see people on the floor kneeling or raising their hands or dancing and clapping. This is so encouraging and refreshing as we see a body of people who love Jesus and love praising him no matter what others think."[18]

Visible response is an earmark of worship. It first appeared when contemporary worship stated to replace traditional, hymn-based worship. Millennial worship leaders have taken it a step farther into a new era of freedom and expression.

Leading Worshippers to God

As I interviewed various worship leaders, I concluded with a summary question: What do you want to experience about God as you lead them in worship? At first blush this may sound redundant, but I am striving to go deeper into the heart attitudes of worship leaders with each question.

John Mendez sees worship as a "refueling opportunity." Young adults have been moving around the Fairfield area all week, and they live in a very high-pressure atmosphere. The pressure to perform is only exceeded by the pressure to conform. In many ways, day-to-day life in this New York City suburb is fraught with maximum stress. Worship at Sanctuary is designed to counteract this stress, to lead people into the presence of the God of all comfort.

"We want people to experience God's glory, and his glory alone," Mendez is single minded about this. "We want to help people take their focus off themselves and put it back on God where it belongs. Worship is not about us. It is about God."[19] Mendez is adamant in insisting that the goal is not some warm and fuzzy emotion. The goal is solely centered on God and all his glory.

"Does the worship room, the atmosphere, distract?" I asked Mendez. He replied that they turn the lights down low to black out both the room and

17. Refvik, email to author, January 24, 2012.
18. Khamarji, email to author, January 20, 2012.
19. Mendez, interview, January 2012.

Vertical Worship—God Centered

the people. They increase the volume to shut out all audible distractions. "It gets me through the week," Mendez insists. Worship is what sustains him and his young family. It is also a constant reminder of the greatness of God.

Chris Brown reveals the evangelistic thrust of Elevation in his answer. "I want people to experience the fullness of God. I want them to be reminded of his faithfulness in their lives." Then he adds, "I want the Holy Spirit to move in special ways in their lives and ours. . . . I want everything that happens to point ultimately to Jesus and the cross and the resurrected life in him."[20]

From Sandals Church across the country in California, Matt Richey makes worship even more personal. For him worship is the vehicle that transports people into the very presence of God. His goal is nothing less than authenticity, "we look forward to seeing where God takes us as we explore what it means to be real in our music."[21]

My roots run deep into worship ministry. For most of my life I engaged in leading worship either personally or as part of a band. Throughout that time I have frequently encountered the temptation to perform. There is something gratifying when people thank you for your work in worship. As I interact with people like John Mendez and Matt Richey it is remarkable to see a lack of the performance mentality. They look with laser clarity at the task of glorifying God and leading others to do this also. This is one of the reasons for investigating an emerging revival within the emerging churches.

From the perspective of a life of worship leadership, Rebecca Refvik underscores this awareness of God's glory. She leads off with an appropriate quotation from William Temple, who served as Archbishop of Canterbury during the tumultuous years of World War II. In response to this question Rebecca Refvik quotes Archbishop Temple's classic statement about worship: "Worship is the submission of all our nature to God. It is the quickening of conscience by His [sic] holiness; the nourishment of mind with His truth; the purifying of imagination by His beauty; the opening of the heart to his love; the surrender of will to His purpose—and all of this gathered up in adoration, the most selfless emotion of which our nature is capable and therefore the chief remedy for that self-centeredness which is our original sin and the source of all actual sin."[22]

Then from her own standpoint Rebecca adds that her primary aim is to make it all about Jesus. "When we connect with God in heartfelt worship,

---

20. Brown, email to author, January 26, 2012.
21. www.sandalschurch.com (accessed January 2012).
22. Refvik, email to author, January 24, 2012.

Emerging Awakening—A Faith Quake

we realize that it is not all about us. It's about the Lord." Explaining this position she applies worship in various circumstances. "When we are weak," Rebecca writes, "one of the best things we can do is worship God." Through worship we return into the very presence of God, "where there is deep joy and true pleasure. Worship causes us to take our eyes off of ourselves and focus and meditate on him." This is the pripary purpose of worship leadership, according to Rebecca.[23]

This exclusive expectation of meeting with the living God seems to characterize worship leaders who have helped me with this chapter. From his experience as a lead singer and worship leader Justin Kendrick expands on these ideas. He speaks of worship as intimate fellowship with God. To illustrate, he quotes the old gospel song, "In the Garden." "The joy we share as we tarry there, none other has ever known."

Kendrick points to the cryptic passage in Matt 28:17. When the disciples met the risen Lord, they worshipped him. Then there is a short phrase: "but some doubted." How could you doubt Jesus, when you are standing face to face with the risen Lord. Kendrick sees such doubt as the most devastating attack on worship. In many ways worship becomes the means by which God overcomes our doubt.

Part of Justin Kendrick's ministry at City Church is Erika Khamarji, an experienced worship leader. "I want people to experience God in a real way," she answers when asked about the goal of leading worship. Then she adds detail. She wants people to experience God for who he really is, as a loving, gracious, merciful God who will forgive mistakes they have made, a God who loves them no matter what is going on in their lives, and a God who is deserving of our praise through worship."[24]

To this powerful manifest of worship, Erika adds even further detail. She remarks that when we raise our hands in worship this is a sign of surrender to the Spirit working within us. She truly believes it is the Spirit who moves people to weep, dance, or laugh. She concludes, "Real worship is truly an incredible experience because of the Holy Spirit." This enables a former worship leader to become a deep worshipper in her life at City Church.

It may be redundant to our work, but I am constantly amazed at the depth of perception exhibited by worship leaders in the emerging church.

---

23. Ibid.
24. Khamarji, email to author, January 20, 2012.

They seem to be taking not only their generation, but indeed the entire Christian community, into a more serious approach to worship.

Perhaps Angela Lear puts it best when she writes: "Our hope is that we will sing songs and play music in such a way that people will experience and see God as high and lofty. [He is] the King of Kings and Lord of Lords who is worthy of all praise and in doing so they recognize that very same God loves them with a passionate and unending love."[25]

In a separate email Angela commented on the ministry of Ron Kenoly. Rehearsal was "incredibly powerful and Christ centered." Then she added this insightful sentence: "I learned through that experience that every single time I open my mouth to sing whether it be in my car, an intense rehearsal, or standing in front of many people not to take it lightly . . . moments of praising a sacred and holy God can occur anytime, anywhere!"[26]

Worship in Perspective

Several lessons emerge from this survey of worship ministry in the emerging church. We have drawn from diverse people living in very different cultures. In a few summary statements we will attempt to draw some conclusions about vertical worship in the emerging church.

Variety of Personalities

Chris Brown from Elevation and Matt Richey at Sandals both represent the new face of Southern Baptist Churches. Perhaps the Southern Baptists have been most effective at adjusting to reach Millennials.

Angela Lear and Rebecca Refvik come to us from independent evangelical churches, although Transformation is linked to the Christian and Missionary Alliance. Erika Khamarji has grown up in an independent church, and she speaks from this non-denominational approach. John Mendez is also part of the same tradition. Justin Kendrick comes from almost a traditional Pentecostal background. The unifying factor is not denomination. It is a commitment to communicate the glory of God to Mosaic generation young people. Thus varied approaches to worship are used to reach audiences in different venues.

---

25. Lear, email to author, January 24, 2012.
26. Ibid.

Generational Connectivity

Gibbs and Bolger note in their encyclopedic work on the emerging church that Mosaic young people want connection to other generations, especially to the builder generation of their grandparents. Nowhere is this more clearly seen than in the matter of worship. When builders can go beyond the volume of the worship and the endurance of standing for 30–45 minutes, they often find a deep connection to emerging worship. Builders appreciate the God-centeredness of Mosaic worship, and they happily sing along with the very moving music. The fact that many worship leaders pointed to other generations is a supporting evidence for this. Many of them were influenced by Brian Houston at Hillsong. Others were encouraged and inspired by Darlene Zscech. Chris Tomlin's name also cropped up in several of the answers.

Perhaps Chris Brown put it best when he explained the mentoring role of Lee McDerment in Anderson, Indiana. Anyone who has served long in ministry can look back at mentors who shaped their lives, and Lee McDerment certainly played that role in developing Chris Brown as a worship leader for the intense atmosphere of Elevation Church in Charlotte, North Carolina.

The intergenerational connectivity is seen most clearly in the worship ministry of emerging churches. These creative young leaders are more than willing to learn, and they seem to value older people whose hearts are right before God and before their young proteges.

Emphasis on Atmosphere

Because of my close personal connection with John Mendez it was possible to probe the issue of atmosphere. Why is the room kept so? What is the volume of the music so loud? His answers were helpful indeed. By keeping the lights down low, distractions are minimal. Also, people feel free to express themselves by raising their hands, kneeling, even dancing as they worship. The volume of the music has a similar effect. It enables people who do not sing well to sing loudly. They have no fear of people hearing them. This reminded me of the Midwestern revival movement in which my family found faith. Many times I stood next to my dad in worship. The shear volume of singing drowned out his monotone, and he felt freedom to worship God at full voice. Worship leading is just that. It is the process by which we encourage others to worship God. The first hurdle to overcome is self-conscious anxiety. When people fee free, they worship freely, and that atmosphere of freedom is the aim of every true worship leader.

Vertical God-Focus

Every aspect of worship leadership must feed into this vertical focus on God. As people lose their inhibitions, they are able to focus their vision on God himself. This is the overarching purpose of all worship. Very often I thank our worship team for "taking me up into the glory." As I enter fully into the worship experience people fade away, the atmosphere becomes secondary, and the music becomes a vehicle for listing my mind and heart heavenward.

It was Mark Detzler who first introduced the term vertical worship. He explained that at City Church in Bristol, England the sole criterion of worship music is this: if it lifts people minds toward God, then it is used. If it focuses on feelings, then it is rejected. As John Mendez put it, "we do not want to create a warm, fuzzy feeling. We want true worship of the eternal God."[27t]

---

27. Mendez, interview, January 2012.

4

Living Belief—No Dead Dogmas

Scott McKnight put it best: "At its core, the emerging movement is an attempt to fashion a new ecclesiology [doctrine of the church]. Its distinctive emphasis can be seen in worship, its concern for orthopraxy, and its missional orientation."[1] Doctrine is a constant source of discussion and even derision among observers of the emerging movement. D. A. Carson set the tone in his book, *Becoming Conversant with the Emerging Church—Understanding a Movement and Its Implications*. Carson focused on the heretical teachings of two writers, Brian McLaren and Steven Chalke.[2] Although Steven Chalke is less known in the United States, he has written shock theology for the British audience, as exemplified by his book, *The Last Message of Jesus*. Brian McLaren is an American pastor with a similar shock approach to traditional Christian truth, as seen in his book *A Generous Orthodoxy*. Carson makes the point that both McLaren and Chalke commit a grievous logical error by retreating to postmodernism for their view of doctrinal truth, rather than the solidity of Scripture and the bedrock of reason.

One might add a further support for Carson's critique. In 2011, Rob Bell released *Love Wins: A Book About Heaven, Hell, and the Fate of Every Person Who Ever Lived*. In this book Bell revived the rather hackneyed arguments against the existence of hell. It gained a lot of publicity for him and propelled him out of the pastorate and into a celebrity career.[3] So, the evidence for heresy within the emerging movement is available, but there

---

1. McKnight, "Five Streams of the Emerging Church."
2. Carson, *Becoming Conversant*, 71–7,
3. Bell, *Love Wins*.

is more evidence for biblical belief. This is not a creed set in stone, but belief clothed in the garb of everyday life. As McKnight emphasizes, here is orthopraxy (proper behavior) above orthodoxy (proper belief).

David Kinnaman released a summary of his book *You Lost Me* on the Barna Group website.[4] In this concise document he lists six reasons why Millennial or Mosaic kids are leaving traditional churches. Several of them relate to doctrinal teaching. It is helpful to remind ourselves of these reasons, as we discuss the doctrinal basis of the emerging movement. Many of the issues raised by Millennials are actually doctrinally based.

First, he notes that churches seem overprotective; they seem to desire that young people will be insulated from the world around them. In a phrase, they believe Christians "demonize everything outside the church."

Second, Kinnaman concluded that teens and twenty-year-olds find evangelical Christianity to be shallow. Ironically, a large majority agreed with the statement: "The Bible is not taught clearly or often enough." This explains the heavy emphasis on Bible teaching among the emerging churches.

Third, churches seem antagonistic toward science. Christians are so intent at keeping the evolution-creation debate alive, that they ignore the scientific questions of the present world.

Fourth, churches are simplistic in teaching about sex. They give no clear guidance to young people who are already sexually active. In an effort to block sexual activity, churches often block out necessary teaching also.

Fifth, Millennials wrestle with the exclusive claims of Christianity. Children perceive the church is afraid of other belief systems, and consequently they do not know what others believe. Furthermore, the church seems to reject other religions without building a solid Scriptural basis for Christian faith.

Sixth, the church is unfriendly to those who doubt. An elderly friend has been uniformly negative in his approach to the emerging church. He believes it is a heresy, perhaps even a sect. Ironically, his young grandson is wrestling with doubts and cannot take them either to his wise, godly grandfather or to the church his family attends.

Scot McKnight adds a further indication of the doctrinal dilemma of the emerging church. He notes that they maintain "post-systematic theology." For centuries, the church has discussed theology in well-worn categories, such as the doctrine of God, the doctrine of revelation, the doctrine of Christ, and the doctrine of the atonement. Great books have

---

4. Kinnaman, "Six Reasons."

been written on systematic theology, many of which have extended to multiple volumes. Some of these theology textbooks were written by solid evangelicals. Among them were Louis Sperry Chafer of Dallas Theological Seminary, Henry Thiessen of Wheaton College, and Wayne Grudem. Of course, others were also written by non-evangelical scholars, such as Karl Barth, Schleiermacher, and Schweitzer. Nonetheless, systematic theology drove theological education in the United States and Western Europe for at least two centuries.

The emerging movement contests the dominance of systematic theology. They believe God did not reveal himself in a list of propositional truths. Rather he revealed himself in a narrative, a story. For this reason emerging pastors cover a broad span of theological perspectives. Mark Driscoll is unabashedly reformed. Justin Kendrick is Arminian. Many espouse an Anabaptist theology, such as Derwin Gray, Bobby Conway, and Steve Furtick.

A powerful assessment of theology comes from Mark Driscoll. In a speech entitled, "Four Points of the Movement," he leads off with a defense of reformed theology. He asserts that all theology must begin with God, not with the human condition. He reminds the listeners that the order of salvation is crucial. God regenerates people before they have the ability to believe. He underlines this with a helpful analogy: "A child is born before it cries." In summarizing the significance of theology, Driscoll adds: "We need to be Christ-centered not just cause-centered."[5]

In a remarkably insightful article in *Telegraph* of London, "Return to Religion," Peter Oborne noted some manifestations of the emerging movement as seen across England, but mainly in London. He noted that pentecostal Christianity is thriving because of African immigrants now living in the United Kingdom. Anglican churches have abandoned the Victorian beauty of historical buildings. Now they meet in movie theaters and other neutral venues. They are trying to reach out to the Mosaics in Britain.

David Stroud heads Christ Church, which meets in the Mermaid Theater in London. Admittedly, his congregation is composed mainly of students and young professional people. Stroud insists: "We preach an orthodox Christian message." Then he confidently claims: "Do that well and you have to lock the doors to keep them out." Amazing as it sounds, it is the Anglican Church that often catches the wave of spiritual interest among Millennial young people in the United Kingdom.[6]

5. Driscoll, "Four Points."
6. Oborne, "Return to Religion."

Living Belief—No Dead Dogmas

The God Who is Real

It is Sandals Church that makes so much of the word, "real." They focus all their efforts on authenticity. They lift authenticity to a prominent position in their mission statement: "Being real with ourselves, God and others."[7] If one aspect of God is important to the emerging movement, it is his authenticity. The Scriptures refer to him as the living God, and by implication they contrast him with dead idols of the world.

Millennial Christ followers are in search of the real thing, and they are very quick to discern the fake. Scot McKnight expresses this in a first person statement: "We believe the Great Tradition offers various ways for telling the truth about God's redemption in Christ, but we don't believe any one theology gets it right."[8] For this reason, you cannot categorize the emerging church. In some expressions, such as Mark Driscoll, it is true to the reformed tradition. Bobby Conway at Life Fellowship in Charlotte is strongly shaped by Dallas Theological Seminary's brand of dispensational theology. Justin Kendrick at City Church traces his roots to classical Pentecostalism, but he goes beyond that tradition in much of his teaching.

All of this prompts me to assert that the emerging movement is shaping an entirely new theology. This is not surprising. When revival swept England in the eighteenth century, a new Wesleyan theology emerged. The same is true of the Reformation, when Luther and Melanchthon hammered out a whole new paradigm of theology. It is not an overstatement to say the Great Awakening in America gave rise to a new theology expressed mainly by Jonathan Edwards.

Derwin Gray summarizes this when he writes: We have "a high and lofty view of God."[9] This promotes a very high view of the Trinity, God the Father, God the Son, and God the Holy Spirit. Then Gray adds orthopraxy to this orthodoxy, when he writes: "All our actions, teaching, prayer, mission, and spiritual transformation will be driven by our view of God." Although this is not traditional theology it is in many ways the epitome of theology.

Those who serve with him at Transformation Church embrace Derwin Gray's assertion. Angela Lear is executive director of the creative team, and she echoes Gray's teaching when she writes: My "main goal in leading

---

7. www.sandalschurch.com (accessed December 15, 2011).
8. McKnight, "Five Streams of the Emerging Church."
9. Gray, email to author, October 5, 2011.

worship is to lead and engage others by personal example as we focus on praising a holy and magnificent God through music."[10]

This tight link between belief and behavior is universal. For many years I have introduced my course on historical theology with this statement: "Every person on the earth lives exactly what they believe." It is my firm conviction that theology is the sole motivator of behavior. For instance, President Bill Clinton explained that a Baptist pastor had told him life begins at birth. This freed Clinton to embrace a pro-abortion political philosophy. He was living exactly what he believed.

The leader of Sanctuary in Fairfield, Connecticut is Josh Feay. Although he lives and works in an evangelical community, he was educated at Yale Divinity School, one of the major bastions of philosophical and theological liberalism. (Please do not read this as a condemnation of Yale. As an erstwhile post-doctoral fellow I have great respect and enthusiasm for Yale).

Feay invests serious thought into the leading of the emerging community Sanctuary. He goes beyond the weekly worship and teaching time to explain the object of community life: "We also connect people to God by surrounding them with God's people in community. We find that people often *feel* God when they are accepted into God's community of the church. So helping people *feel* God's community is important to our worship [italics mine]."

Did you notice how Josh Feay elevates the concept of "feeling" in his statement about Sanctuary's purpose? This is particularly important for postmodern young people. They want to experience God more than they want a long list of propositional statements about God. This affects not only worship, but also preaching, which is geared to introduce people into a living experience with God. As the old Southern preacher put it: "The gospel is better 'felt' than 'tellt.'"

If Josh Feay grasps the emotional and experiential impact of God on a person's life, Zenzo Matoga is even more forceful. Zenzo calls his ministry, United Night of Worship, and he is committed to using worship as a vehicle to teach deep lessons about God. Zenzo writes: "I hear the sound of the abundance of rain!" He relies on the words of the Prophet Elijah, as revival swept Israel on Mt. Carmel (1 Kings 18:41). Then Zenzo adds explanation: "that sound is the sound of prayers from all those in New England that are seeking God in desperation. It's the sound of HOPE for all those who still believe that the God of Light will triumph over all darkness!"[11]

---

10. Lear, email to author, December 27, 2011.
11. Matoga, www.facebook.com (accessed May 2, 2011).

Zenzo uses Facebook as a main means of communication with his circle of worshippers around New England. This is very much a generational matter. The Mosaics are moved much more by Facebook communication than by any other means of connectivity. In many ways, the emerging movement is teaching the church at large to use the social media as deliberate discipleship tools.

When we turn to the runaway ministry of Steven Furtick at Elevation Church his theological conservatism amazes us. He explains the Trinity in three statements: "The Father—God is great, God is good. The Son—God became man. The Holy Spirit—God is always present." Notice the conservative expression of Furtick, who admits it when he says: "Although our approach is anything but traditional, we believe in and maintain a conservative theological position."[12] This moves me to a preliminary conclusion, that the emerging movement is a revival within the framework of previous, biblical movements. It does not represent a disjuncture from the past.

Perhaps one of the most concise statements concerning the person of God comes from a sermon by Justin Kendrick. The setting was anything but traditional, as several hundred young adults packed Toad's Place, a rocking music venue in downtown New Haven, Connecticut. Justin Kendrick took the crowd straight to God, when he said: "God is good. He created us to be good, but we rebelled. This opened a wide separation between us and a good God. You can't control your life. Separation keeps us from joy." Then with the instincts of an evangelist Justin went straight to the gospel: "Because God is good he must judge sin. So we must have a Savior."[13]

The trappings of worship may sound strange and shocking to us. The message of the emerging movement is couched in different words, but the meat of the message is the same. It is the age-old Bible phrase: "Be reconciled to God" (2 Cor 5:19–20).

Biblical Reality in an Unreal Age

The emerging movement has a fresh approach to the Scriptures. There is a refreshing return to biblical preaching among some of the emerging pastors. One of the strongest and most influential is Mark Driscoll at Mars Hill Church in Seattle. Recently he released an online sermon titled, "Ten Painful Lessons from the Early Days of Mars Hill Church." The second lesson

12. www.elevationchurch.org (accessed December 15, 2011).
13. Kendrick, Christmas at Toad's Place sermon, December 18, 2011.

addressed the reality that a pastor must, "lead from the pulpit." In the wake of the culture wars in the United States during the 1960s and 1970s many pastors were intimidated. Seminaries even produced a generation of preachers who were cautious, almost reticent to take leadership. The result was a generation of lead pastors who preached to the crowd, and tried to say what the crowd wanted to hear. Their style of pastoral ministry also reflected this. Lead pastors retreated to their studies and hired so-called care pastors to interface with the congregation. Consequently, a leadership gap developed in the church. The Mosaic generation sensed this and abandoned evangelicalism to a great degree, as demonstrated by Kinnaman's book, *You Lost Me*.

Driscoll speaks for a new generation of pastors who are leaders, and he believes leadership must come from the pulpit. Driscoll summarizes: "For our church to grow and for me to survive, I needed to transition from being everyone's pastor to being a missiologist preacher who led the church from the Bible in the pulpit. As we trained and installed elders and deacons, I transitioned many of these pastoral duties to other qualified leaders and began focusing more on developing the vision and mission of Mars Hill, studying the Bible, praying, and preaching."[14]

Scot McKnight discusses the preaching of the emerging movement and concludes that it is "prophetic (or at least provocative)." The emerging pastors challenge the status quo of evangelicalism, and many of them bring biblical truth with an edge to it. Sometimes their preaching makes traditionalists uncomfortable.[15]

Having said that, most of the emerging church pastors are biblical in their approach. Derwin Gray summarizes it in a response to our question: "What shapes your preaching?" He answered: "We are committed, by the Spirit's enabling power, to develop a biblical, servant-hearted community . . . We will teach and live biblical financial stewardship." Gray laces each point of his manifesto for Transformation Church with reference to the Bible. He believes the Bible is the sole basis upon which they must operate.

Perhaps the most thoughtful response to my question about biblical bases of the emerging movement came from Josh Feay, who leads Sanctuary in Fairfield, Connecticut. Remember that Josh did his theological studies in the eclectic atmosphere of Yale Divinity School, and he has wrestled with the issues that define church life in the emerging movement. I would argue that Josh Feay may be one of the most thoughtful sources of information

14. Driscoll, "Ten Painful Lessons."
15. McKnight, "Five Streams of the Emerging Church."

Living Belief—No Dead Dogmas

for the project at hand. He asserted that people "feel God" as they participate in the community live, a vibrant aspect of Sanctuary. Then he adds, "We also connect people to God through the Bible, which is God's written word to us. We do that mainly through preaching."[16] Here again, the aspect of pastoral leadership comes into focus. The Sanctuary leadership team is fully aware that their job is leading people into an ever-deepening relationship with God through Jesus Christ.

Josh Feay writes from the rough and tumble atmosphere of largely secular New England. Steven Furtick, on the other hand, speaks out of the erstwhile Bible Belt of Charlotte, North Carolina. In fact, one observer referred to Charlotte as "the buckle on the Bible Belt." Furtick tries to bridge the gap between postmodern culture and biblical Christianity. He admits, "Elevation Church aggressively reaches out to people who are far from God. Rather than run from the culture, we have chosen to harness it to connect with people and show them God's timeless truths." The basic conservatism of Elevation shines through when Furtick adds: "Although our approach is anything but traditional, we believe in and maintain a conservative theological position."[17]

We recall that Furtick is a graduate of Southern Baptist Seminary in Louisville, Kentucky. While there he was trained under the leadership of Al Moehler, one of the strongest voices in America for the neo-Reformed movement. Furtick's funky appearance and style are really an appearance adopted to open doors to Millennial young people, and it works amazingly well.

When one reads the doctrinal statement of Elevation Church, it sounds incredibly conservative: "The Bible is God's Word to all people. It was written by human authors under the supernatural guidance of the Holy Spirit. Because it was inspired by God, the Bible is truth without any mixture of error and is completely relevant to our daily lives."[18] This resounding statement of inerrancy is followed by an extensive list of biblical citations. At this point it is helpful to note that the City Church doctrinal statement in New Haven closely parallels this declaration from Elevation. A commitment to the inerrancy of Scripture helps explain the unusual power both Steven Furtick and Justin Kendrick demonstrate in their preaching.

Sandals Church in Riverside, California is part of the same Southern Baptist movement as Elevation Church. It is amazing, therefore, that Sandals softens its statement about Scripture. After asserting that the Bible

---

16. Feay, email to author, November 2, 2011.
17. www.elevationchurch.org (accessed December 15, 2011).
18. Ibid.

is written under inspiration from God, the Sandals statement adds: "It is completely true *in all that it affirms*. It is the source of God's divine revelation and is the final authority for our belief and practice [italics mine]."[19]

Following in the wake of the Lausanne Conference of 1974 the phrase, "in all that it affirms," was added to manly doctrinal statements. It seems to soften the commitment to plenary (complete), verbal (word for word), inspiration.

Arising from the Reformed Baptist tradition in England, Bristol City Centre Church has an unusually strong statement about Scripture in its doctrinal statement, a statement shared with the mother church, Kensington Baptist Church: "God has revealed himself in the Bible, which consists of Old and New Testaments alone (this excludes the Apocrypha). Every word was inspired by God through human authors, so the Bible as originally given is in its entirety the Word of God, without error and fully reliable in fact and doctrine."

Although the worship is loud and raucous at times, many emerging churches hold a strong view of Scripture. Lead pastors preach a biblical message clothed for missiological purposes in the culture of twenty-first century young people. They speak the unchanging truth of God's word into the shifting sands of postmodern philosophy.

Jesus: More than an Example

From time immemorial, some theologians have seen Jesus as a good man, a moral example. However, the death and resurrection of Christ rule out forever the condescending claim that Jesus is just a good man.

Ironically, when Mark Driscoll and Gerry Breshears write their influential book, *Vintage Jesus*, they quote Billy Graham, a ninety-year-old evangelist of a bygone era. In is an excerpt from a *Newsweek* interview granted by Billy Graham after his ninetieth birthday, the old evangelist says: "Jesus was not just another great religious teacher, nor was he only another in a long line of individuals seeking after spiritual truth. He was, instead, truth itself. He was God incarnate."[20]

The significance of Driscoll and Breshears's work cannot be underestimated. The person of work has been attacked by radical theologians in the emerging movement. For instance, Steven Chalke attacked the concept of

19. www.sandalschurch.com (accessed January 12, 2012).
20. Driscoll and Breshears, *Vintage Jesus*, 19.

substitutionary atonement. He asserted that if God allowed his Son to be sacrificed on a cross, this would be cosmic child abuse. Biblical scholars and preachers rose up to condemn this blasphemy, but the fact remains.[21] Theologians such as Chalke claim they are simply "pushing the envelope," taking Christian belief to its logical extreme. Nevertheless, they are compromising seriously the Christian message in doing so. The secular media gladly pounce on such pronouncements.

When we turn to the young pastors, a different picture soon emerges. Seldom in my fifty years of ministry have I ever heard a more powerful preacher than Justin Kendrick in New Haven, Connecticut. He is at his best when he explains the atonement of Christ to postmodern listeners. At a Christmas event in a music hall near Yale's campus Kendrick put it clearly: "God created us to be good, but we rebelled. This led to separation from God. You cannot control your life. This separation from God robs us of joy. The good news is that there is a Savior, who is Christ."[22] Kendrick went on to explain in detail the fact that Jesus died to pay for our sin, to reconcile us to God. And this was a Christmas celebration.

In the faith commitment of City Church they state unequivocally that, "Jesus is the only plan for bringing people who are enemies of God back into a right relationship with God." Then they add: "He defeated death in His resurrection so that we could have life."

At Bristol City Centre Church in Bristol, England there is also a clear comprehension of the atonement. Remember, England is Chalke's home field, and he has influenced many theologians and preachers in England. Still, Bristol City Centre Church stands true when they insist: "The Lord Jesus Christ is fully God and fully man.... On the cross He died in the place of sinners, bearing God's punishment for their sin, redeeming them with His blood."[23] This ringing affirmation of the historical belief in substitutionary atonement is embraced by young listeners, who are heartily sick of the cute quips of compromised academics.

This commitment to a biblical perspective on substitutionary atonement is not an isolated viewpoint. It is not limited to the east coast or to traditional England. From Riverside, California the statement of Sandals Church is particularly strong: "Jesus lived a perfect life and died as a

---

21. Carson, *Becoming Conversant*, 185.
22. Kendrick, Christmas at Toad's Place sermon, December 18, 2011.
23. www.kenbaptist.org (accessed January 31, 2012).

Emerging Awakening—A Faith Quake

sacrifice for the sins of the world. He rose bodily from the grave three days after being buried to display His victory over sin."[24]

Near the Sandals campus is also the campus of California Baptist University (CBU). When I investigated this university it amazed me. After forty plus years in the academic world I was astounded by the criteria for selecting faculty. The application form included all of the necessary academic data, and then a final question was added: "If a student came to you and asked to become a believer in Jesus Christ, could you lead them to saving faith?" This is one more piece of evidence for the commitment of a Millennial generation to spiritual authenticity. Even their professors need to be real in their life of faith.

At the heart of the Bible Belt, Elevation Church calls its crowd to an affirmation of the unique person and work of Jesus Christ. "Jesus is completely human but, at the same time, completely God. He is the *only plan* for bringing people who are far from God back into a right relationship with God. . . . He lived a perfect life, so that he could be a substitution for us in satisfying God's demands for perfection. He defeated death in His resurrection so that we could have life [italics mine]."[25]

Recently, one young apologist posted a caustic critique of Elevation Church. His argument in a nutshell was this: The church is ordained by God to teach believers. Elevation Church emphasized evangelism. Therefore, Elevation Church is not a real church. To this I would answer: Elevation teaches the "whole counsel of God" (Acts 20:27). In so doing, they are reaching the Mosaic generation with a complete gospel and launching new believers into a responsible life of discipleship.

Transformation Church fleshes out the goal of reaching a new generation with the good news of Jesus Christ and his atoning and saving power. They express their purpose to seek out "the wounded, the broken-hearted, and marginalized so that they can be transformed by the Gospel of grace into the image of Jesus joining Him in His mission to transform the world."[26]

When we read the material from Transformation Church it tells volumes about Derwin Gray, the lead pastor. He graduated from Brigham Young University and went straight to the National Football League. While playing in Indianapolis, a zealously evangelistic lineman led Derwin and his wife to faith. They embarked immediately on a program of intense Bible

24. www.sandalschurch.com (accessed January 12, 2012).
25. www.elevationchurch.org (accessed December 15, 2012).
26. Grey, email to author, October 5, 2011.

Living Belief—No Dead Dogmas

study, and later he completed a seminary degree after being transferred to the Carolina Panthers. He is persistent in preaching in depth to his young congregation, because he wants to ensure they will stand strong for the Lord in a postmodern world.

Perhaps we can leave the last word on the role of Jesus in the emerging movement to Mark Driscoll. He has written several books to train new believers as they become part of Mars Hill Church in Seattle. None is more important than *Vintage Jesus*. "Even Jesus' enemies were equally clear that Jesus refused to be considered merely a good man. They wanted to kill Jesus because he was 'making himself equal with God.'"[27]

Is the Holy Spirit Only a Ghost?

Too often evangelicals have cast the trinity as God the Father, God the Son, and the Bible. For many years the Holy Spirit was excluded from evangelical circles for fear that the church might spin out of control. There was a dread of dancing in the aisles, raising hands in worship, and speaking in other tongues.

Ironically, it is the most theologically reformed voice of the emerging church, Mark Driscoll, who throws the windows and doors open to the Holy Spirit. Driscoll attacks the concept of cessationism. Grudem defines cessationism in this way: "Cessationist refers to someone who thinks that certain miraculous spiritual gifts ceased long ago." Grudem further defines the gifts as prophecy, tongues, healings, and casting our demons.[28] Driscoll castigates cessationism. He claims a direct link between Enlightenment atheism, deism, and cessationism. He views cessationism as a denial of God's activity within the time/space world at this time. Driscoll sums it up in one short sentence: "Cessationism is worldliness."[29]

Just as Jesus was filled with the Holy Spirit at his baptism, so we must be filled with the Holy Spirit in order to reach the Millennial generation, according to Driscoll. He sums it up: "We need to be filled like Jesus."[30]

As a lifelong theologian of the evangelical movement, I must confess I have never read such a strong attack against cessationism as Driscoll brings. It is good to remember he was speaking before a group of leaders and pastors

---

27. Driscoll and Breshears, *Vintage Jesus*, 19.
28. Grudem, *Systematic Theology*, 1031.
29. Driscoll, "Four Points."
30. Ibid.

from the Resurgence movement. Resurgence is a loose confederation of emerging leaders Driscoll has put together for the sake of mentoring them.

It is interesting to compare with Driscoll's dramatic statement the statement of City Church in New Haven. Justin Kendrick comes out of a fairly typical Pentecostal background, but the doctrinal statement is rather bland. Under God the Holy Spirit, Kendrick writes: "His presence assures us of our relationship with Christ. He guides believers into all truth and exalts Christ. He convicts people of their sin, God's righteousness, and coming judgment. He comforts us, gives us spiritual gifts, and makes us more like Christ."[31]

In reality, Kendrick takes a stronger view of the Holy Spirit's work. Each week he encourages the prayer team in a healing and deliverance ministry. Singing in the Spirit is part of worship at City Church. Kendrick is completely committed to a ministry of deliverance from demonic control, a crucial element in any emerging church.

The practice of "toning down" statements about the Holy Spirit is also seen in the Elevation statement of faith: "His presence assured us of our relationship with Christ. He guides believers into all truth and exalts Christ." This sounds very much like the City Church statement. When it comes to spiritual gifts, Elevation's statement asserts: "He comforts us, gives us spiritual gifts, and makes us more like Christ."[32] Remember, Elevation pastor Steven Furtick was trained under well-known Reformed theologian, Al Mohler, at Southern Baptist theological Seminary in Louisville. Historically, the Reformed movement has been skeptical of miraculous spiritual signs. Can this be the reason for an implied cessationism in many of the doctrinal statements from emerging churches?

Historically, the American Reformed movement has been cessationist. This goes back to a book written by B. B. Warfield, a Princeton theologian. Warfield's book is titled, *Counterfeit Miracles*, and he refutes the use of charismatic gifts in the modern church.[33]

Having noted the divergence between Driscoll and cessationism, it is interesting to see that some emerging churches make no mention at all of spiritual gifts. For instance, Bristol City Centre Church in Bristol, England takes its doctrinal statement from the parent church, Kensington Baptist Church. Kensington is a keystone church in the reformed Fellowship of

---

31. City Church, "Ministry Government and Structure." Unpublished factsheet. 2012.
32. www.elevationchurch.org (accessed December 15, 2012).
33. Grudem, *Systematic Theology*, 1043 n49.

Independent Evangelical Churches in England. Its doctrinal statement regards the Holy Spirit as comforter and energizer of ministry, but there is no mention whatsoever of spiritual gifts.

Sandals Church is part of the Southern Baptist Convention in California. It likewise emphasizes the empowering and illuminating work of the Holy Spirit in the life of believers. Then the Sandals statement adds: "By the Holy Spirit, believers have spiritual gifts that they use to serve the local church."[34] This is a fairly standard Baptist statement about the Holy Spirit, and it deftly dances around the issue of cessationism.

When we turn to Transformation Church in South Carolina, there is an interesting twist to the teaching about the Holy Spirit. Many of the core values of the church are introduced with this phrase: "through the Holy Spirit's enabling power." Again, Transformation takes a soft approach to the matter of spiritual gifts, especially the miraculous gifts of healing, tongues, and prophecy.

So there remains no question about the person of the Holy Spirit. He is the third person of the Trinity. The matter of spiritual gifts, however, seems to be a matter of some ambiguity among emerging church leaders. Scot McKnight shrouds the whole subject in academic jargon when he writes: "Hence, a trademark feature of the emerging movement is that we believe all theology will remain a conversation about the Truth who is God in Christ through the Spirit, and about God's story of redemption at work in the church. No systematic theology can be final."[35]

In broader cross-section of emerging churches there are remnants of the charismatic movement. Eddie Gibbs and Ryan Bolger notice the influence of John Wimber and the Third Wave Charismatics, and some of the emerging churches follow this pattern. There was a strong emphasis on speaking in tongues within the followers of Wimber. Gibbs and Bolger note that virtually all of the leaders of the emerging movement in the United Kingdom came out of the Third Wave Charismatic camp. This is not true in the United States, where many leaders come from more traditional evangelical backgrounds.[36]

It is my opinion that the breadth of evangelical theology from Arminian to Reformed will continue to be represented in the emerging church. Also,

---

34. www.sandalschurch.com (accessed January 12, 2012).
35. McKnight, "Five Streams of the Emerging Church."
36. Gibbs and Bolger, *Emerging Churches*, 219–20.

the traditional patterns of belief about the Holy Spirit, from cessationism to full acceptance of the gifts, will be present in the emerging movement.

Church that is Missional

We have noted throughout this book that a dominant drive of emerging churches is missional transformation. In many ways it is activity that defines the emerging church, rather than either worship or preaching. What the church does in community seems more important than what the church does in any given worship context. This is where revival is most evident in the emerging movement.

Pastors have become missiologists. Instead of feeding the flock, pastors are firing up the flock to reach outside the doors. Nowhere is this more obvious than in New Haven. Justin Kendrick birthed the idea of City Church in a series of events embracing the whole city of New Haven. On a hot summer day, City Church welcomed more than 1,400 folks for a time of free food and fun. It was a get-to-know-you event. Soon they followed up with a block party. Young and old mingled as missional members of the City Church community welcomed friends new and old. Although there was no formal preaching that day, there was no doubt City Church was hosting the party as a means to win new friends.

To touch the Yale University community, City Church has hosted events at Toad's Place, a music venue adjacent to the Yale campus. Even the regular meeting place for the church is almost on the Yale campus, a sincere sign of welcome to the student community. Justin Kendrick clearly states the goal: "We started City Church to see actual change in the city of New Haven."

The missional aspect of City Church is typical of the outward-looking approach of the emerging movement. Elevation Church plans to conquer Charlotte for the Christian message. "Elevation Church aggressively reaches out to people who are far from God," they admit. Then they explain it: "Rather than run from culture, we have chosen to harness it to connect with people and show them God's timeless truths."[37] Elevation has grown by leaps and bounds, and it has managed this growth by creating campuses all over the Charlotte area. Growth is the constant at Elevation.

Sandals Church takes its inspiration from Rick Warren, a neighboring pastor. His "purpose-driven church" is their model for ministry. Although the model is well-known the pattern is adapted to reach Mosaic young

---

37. www.elevationchurch.org (accessed December 15, 2012).

Living Belief—No Dead Dogmas

adults. Sandals sends a message of authenticity, and this draws young adults into the circle with amazing success. Sandals Church has a single focus for communal ministry. They are vigorous in their efforts to eradicate human trafficking in their state and the world. Modern slavery begins with the promise of a job and becomes forced labor or debt servitude. Sandals Church throws its full weight against this sleazy slave network.

Missional transformation also drives the ministry of Sanctuary in Fairfield, Connecticut. Sanctuary embraces the motto: "We seek to love God, love people, and serve our world."[38] This compels many Sanctuary members to engage in urban ministries in the nearby city of Bridgeport, Connecticut. Sanctuary also sponsors several worldwide mission ministries each year.

Mark Detzler is a former missionary pastor. He led an emerging church model in suburban Rome, Italy. After returning to the United Kingdom he took up the cause of refugees, as consecutive waves of displaced people came ashore in the British Isles. This involved teaching them English, homework clubs for their kids, helping them find jobs, and often pleading their cases in court. He now serves as co-director of an English as Second Language program at a local community college. From this involvement it was a short step to city center Bristol. Young adults, the Millennial generation, were moving into city center. Most came because of studies at the university or jobs in the city. Mark Detzler notices that many of the Anglican churches no longer had services. In fact, their doors were locked shut. So, Mark and Cathy launched Bristol City Center Church. The entire operation is missional in character as they seek connections with the community through jazz nights, social events, and a very open meeting place in the heart of the community.

Mark Driscoll coined the phrase, "missiologist preacher." He summarized it in this statement: "For our church to grow and for me to survive, I needed to transition from being everyone's pastor to being a missiologist preacher who led the church from the Bible in the pulpit." This likewise shaped Driscoll's description of the church: "In addition to raising and training up leaders in official church positions such as elder and deacon, we also made it clear that our members were expected to be missionaries and to do the work of the ministry in their daily lives."[39]

Driscoll sees the emerging church as a missional church. People in the church must always be missionaries, and the pastor is a missiologist. An

---

38. Feay, email to author, December 27, 2011.
39. Driscoll, "Ten Painful Lessons."

explanation might be helpful at this point. Traditionally, missiologists have trained people to serve God in other cultures, in cross-cultural ministries. The emerging movement has realized our culture is no longer a Christian culture. Rather, in the postmodern generation there is a prevailing secular spirit that finds Christianity foreign, even frightening. So it is important to remember that the church, according to Driscoll, is both "sent and sending." The church is sent to its community as a missionary people. This is the so-called great commission of Jesus, going into every culture to make disciples (Matt. 28:18–20).

McKnight emphasizes the missional nature of emerging churches. The "praxis stream (of the emerging movement) is being *missional*." This is the ministry of reconciliation to which Paul referred in 2 Cor 5:18. The church is God's means of reconciling the world to himself. McKnight then adds that missional activity participates in redemptive work within the community. God works through the vibrant and vital church community to touch the culture and to give credibility to the gospel.

The church also participates in the holistic redemptive work of God in the world. The Spirit groans and the very creation groans (Rom 8:18–27) in anticipation of renewal, and the emerging church is part of this renewal movement.

The holistic model of missional activity flows directly from the model of Jesus's life and ministry. He combined healing, deliverance, feeding the hungry, challenging the authorities, and even raising up the dead. His ministry was not simply teaching and preaching. So it must be with the church. The church must be known by what it does, not simply for what it claims to be. Scot McKnight summarizes with this statement about Jesus: "He cared, in other words, not just about lost souls, but also about whole persons and whole societies."[40]

Orthopraxy Versus Orthodoxy

For a hundred years, we evangelicals have fought theological battles. When the inerrancy of Scripture was challenged by German liberalism, we rose up to resist the attack. We marshaled our best forces to define and defend the inerrancy of the Bible. When the teaching of Jesus Christ came into question by critical historical Jesus questions, we fought them toe-to-toe. We asserted the biblical and historical doctrine of the incarnation. We affirmed

40. McKnight, "Five Streams of the Emerging Church."

Living Belief—No Dead Dogmas

that Jesus is all God and all man, the God-Man. When the atonement of Jesus was questioned, we stood in the gap again. During my school days, liberal theologians smeared our adherence to the substitutionary atonement. They called it "slaughter house religion." More recently, Steven Chalke has put down the substitutionary atonement as "cosmic child abuse," God subjecting his Son Jesus to humiliation and crucifixion.

Now we have a new generation, the Millennial or Mosaic generation. They are not scarred by the same battles. They have never faced the withering attacks my generation has. They seek to win their world for Jesus, and they do this by replacing orthodoxy (proper belief) with orthopraxy (proper behavior). The means by which Millennials communicate to their world can be summarized in one word: authenticity. As the Sandals Church community phrases it: "Real with self, real with God, and real with others."[41] They want to show the world around them what Christ followers look like. Scot McKnight says this has led to a new view of the church, a new ecclesiology, or doctrine of the church. "Its distinctive emphases can be seen in its worship, its concern with orthopraxy, and its missional orientation."[42]

This leads the emerging movement to amazing innovation. Some of which may seem fraught with risk, but all of which seems to exemplify the life of Jesus Christ. Perhaps we might conclude by citing a few examples of such missional living.

City Church in New Haven values the community life of its core group. For this reason, several have purchased large houses in the Westfield section of the city. Married couples rent parts of the houses to single members of the church community. This strengthens the fiber of fellowship while creating a natural accountability network.

Since Sandals Church is located near university campuses they have dedicated one staff pastor to the campus ministry. Justin Pardee fills that role, and he has a deep commitment to the task of discipling the students who come to be part of Sandals.

In Peter Oborne's piece for the *Telegraph* in London, he mentions several innovative approaches to church in the city of London. One of them is St. Mary's. Located in the Islington district of London, St. Mary's melds both young professional people and the traditional London working class. Oborne notes, "These two groups rarely come together—but they do so at

---

41. www.sandalschurch.com (accessed January 12, 2012).
42. McKnight, "Five Streams of the Emerging Church."

Emerging Awakening—A Faith Quake

St. Mary's, which provides the model of a church which grows by building up its links with the local community."[43]

Bristol City Center Church has carved out a niche through intensive, immediate pastoral care. The communal fabric of the church has been both tested and strengthened as families faced critical points in their lives. Mark and Cathy Detzler have devoted themselves to building relationships that knit together the community of faith, and together they become a safe haven for people who join the fellowship.

Kevin Butterfield has emphasized revival in his ministry at Melbourne, Australia. He builds bridges to pastors from other faith traditions in order to kindle revival among them. In fact, he calls his ten-week training program, "fire-starters." They seek to strengthen prayer ministry by introducing healing and deliverance ministries. This is a remarkable outreach for Vineyard ministry, because it spreads the spiritual insights that have driven their work since the time of John Wimber.

In Zurich, we encountered International Christian Fellowship (ICF). More than two thousand attend the eight services every weekend at ICF. At first it appears each crowd is too big, too impersonal. Afterward, however, there is very lively community fellowship. A well-stocked food court provides the relaxed atmosphere for meaningful encounter.

Zenzo Matoga is, first and foremost, a worship leader, but he harbors a passion for revival. He senses a rising tide of renewal in New England, and this engenders a spirit of hope throughout the region. Zenzo has hope, because he believes that "the God of Light will triumph over all darkness."[44]

The emerging movement is outward looking, as we will discover in the next chapter. Whenever and wherever you encounter them, there is a passion to see God at work in their community. True enough, they often focus on one city or one region. However, the quest to see God glorified is the glorious meaning of missional transformation.

---

43. Oborne, "Return to Religion."
44. Matoga, www.facebook.com (accessed May 2, 2011).

5

Why the Church is Emerging

AS IS SO OFTEN the case, a new movement arises because of the poverty of the old. For instance, when the Catholic Church could not achieve reform in its famous reforming councils of the fourteenth and fifteenth centuries, the Protestant Reformation affected reform at the cost of division. When American Christianity slumped into a slough of deism during the colonial era, the Great Awakening under Jonathan Edwards called it back to vital faith. Several decades later, Timothy Dwight lamented the loss of faith at Yale when he assumed the presidency, and his preaching ignited the Second Great Awakening. We recall that Timothy Dwight was the grandson of Jonathan Edwards. Yale was known as an open market for ideas, so revival found a fertile field there. I have studied campus revivals in depth and discovered that many awakening movements began on or near university centers.

In the 1960s, denominational churches in America were locked in a fortress mentality, and the Jesus People tried to pry open the door for a new generation. Chuck Smith caught this trend and founded the Calvary Chapel movement. It ignited an awakening of sorts among the Jesus People and the Baby Boomers at large. This can be seen in the ministry of preachers like Greg Laurie at Riverside, California, and also Bob Dyer in Ft. Lauderdale, Florida.

By the same token, the emerging movement views historical evangelical churches as either dead or dying. The worship and ministry of the so-called contemporary worship movement does not speak to the Millennial generation. They feel doctrinal purity has suffocated spiritual life and fragmented community consciousness. Perhaps it is easy to understand, because the contemporary worship movement of the 1980s and 1990s was peopled by the parents of Millennial or Mosaic young people.

Emerging Awakening—A Faith Quake

Now the emerging movement searches for true authenticity. As city Church in New Haven puts it: "Authentic: Finding Real in a Culture of Fake."[1] I would argue that this is, to some degree, a generational issue. Young adults are trying desperately to individuate, to create a lifestyle different from their parents. This is a sociological phenomenon of the twentieth century, and it is pronounced in all the generations of that century: Builders (born prior to 1946), Baby Boomers (born 1946–1964), Generation X or Gen-X (born 1965–1980), and Millennials or Generation Y (born 1980–89).

I would argue the idea of individuation from parental models is a phenomenon of the middle-to-late twentieth century. To explain, there is separation from parents both in terms of living nearby and doing the same job as their parents. The Builder generation was the first generation to attend college en masse, and this often led them to geographical as well as vocational separation from their parents. It is within this sociological context we can begin to understand the emerging church movement. Eddie Gibbs, Ryan Bolger, and David Kinnaman have factored these basic sociological systems into their assessments of the emerging movement.[2]

Scot McKnight calls the emerging movement, "post-evangelical." To quote McKnight: "It is post-evangelical in the way that neo-evangelicalism (in the late 1950s) was post-fundamentalist." With the deft hand of a creative scholar, McKnight coins the term "postmodern evangelicalism." He sees the emerging movement as coming to grips with a generation whose philosophical tendency is postmodernism.[3]

Even in England this mindset is gaining traction. The *Telegraph* piece pertaining to an increase in church attendance notices something of an emerging approach to church. The rather hidebound Anglican Church has realized they cannot hold up in the fortress of Victorian vaulted churches. The church must be among the people if it will be of the people. For this reason creative young vicars, many of who are evangelical, are experimenting with new forms of worship. Giles Fraser resigned as Canon of St. Paul's Cathedral in London, because he protested the harsh treatment of the Occupy movement (this is akin to the "Occupy Wall Street" action in New York).

According to the journalist Peter Oborne, Giles "argues that a hunger for spirituality and meaning lies behind the recent rise in church attendances." He is supported strongly by a key evangelical, Bishop James Jones

---

1. This is an unpublished handout from City Church in New Haven, CT (2011).
2. Kinnaman, "Six Reasons." Gibbs and Bolger, *Emerging Churches*.
3. McKnight, "Five Streams of the Emerging Church."

of Liverpool. Bishop James claims: "People are aware there is a big shift in society coming along, even though they might not understand it. So I'm not surprised that the ground is now more fertile for the spread of the Christian message."[4]

Justin Kendrick speaks from the heart of the Millennial generation. He is in many ways the epitome of Mosaic church leadership. Having begun his ministry in the field of worship leadership, Justin Kendrick founded in 2011 City Church in New Haven, Connecticut. When I sat down with him, he expressed his passion in these words: "I want to see the Millennial generation moved by the gospel."[5] He gently chided the church of his parents' generation by reminding me that they had established the CEO model of church leadership. The pastor was cast in the mold of a chief executive officer. Now, according to Justin, it is time to turn back the clock and recast the pastor as a servant, a "minister" so to speak. The hallmark of this new generation of church leaders, known as lead pastors, is authenticity or realism. They reject resoundingly the older models of ministry.

John Mendez refers to Francis Chan as a model of the new lead pastor. Chan founded Cornerstone Community Church in Simi Valley, California. Chan was trained in the strong Reformed atmosphere of John MacArthur's Master's College and Seminary. In 2010 he resigned from Cornerstone Church to devote his efforts to ministry in San Francisco. Chan is committed to challenge the skeptical Millennial generation with the truth of Jesus Christ. His incredibly sacrificial lifestyle is attractive to other Millennial leaders, who are trying to capture the model of true servant-leadership.

So, how can we explain the rise of the emerging movement? I suggest that there are at least five areas of contrast between the Boomer sand the Millennials, when it comes to worship. They are these:

1. From CEO to servant leader—who leads them.
2. From fake to real—how they are perceived.
3. From stand up to sing out—what worship is.
4. From missionary to missional—why they exist.
5. From sanctuary to spaces—where they gather.

---

4. Oborne, "The Return to Religion."
5. Interview with Justin Kendrick, July 14, 2011.

Does this sound like a reporter's notebook? Perhaps it is. Parallel to my academic career, I have spent fifty years as a freelance journalist, including work for the venerable British Broadcasting Corporation as a radio commentator.

From CEO to Servant Leader

When I taught at Trinity Evangelical Divinity School in Chicago, one of my courses was "theological education in the developing world." Many foreign students attended this course. Each semester I devoted one lecture to the concept of servant leadership. A young Latin leader accosted me. "I can't do that," he fumed. "In Latin America leaders must be macho men." That day I began to realize how foreign the biblical idea of servant leadership was.

Justin Kendrick describes the role of senior pastor as "team leader." He is not a boss. He is a servant. For this reason, before Kendrick launched City Church he worked for five years building his team. He started with his band Out of Hiding. Patiently, he discipled and prayed with this close-knit group, and this laid a solid basis for the beginning of a church ministry.

In fact, when emerging churches fail to survive, it is usually due to a lack of cohesion among the core group. The lone-ranger approach to pastoral leadership is a guarantee of failure. Every successful emerging church pastor is an excellent team builder.

David Kinnaman underscores this when he writes about lead pastors. He describes the emergence of servant leaders as "the new normal." Church leaders work best with young families—married couples with young children. These families are free to explore new avenues of church life. He concludes: "The world of young adults is changing in significant ways, such as their remarkable access to the world and worldviews via technology, their alienation from various institutions, and their skepticism toward external sources of authority, including Christianity and the Bible."[6]

Notice that Kinnaman speaks of a "new normal." This marks the perceived shift from the business model, the CEO pastor, to a servant leadership model for senior ministers. Notice that I call this a "perceived" shift. It would be erroneous to generalize and claim that all previous pastors had followed the CEO model.

From England the journalist, Peter Oborne, echoes this shift in leadership. In earlier generations, the Church of England vicar was cast as a

6. Kinnaman, "Six Reasons."

Why the Church is Emerging

man out of touch with reality, like Father McKenzie of Beatles fame. He was "writing a sermon for no one to hear." In the Millennial generation Oborne notes that vicars, clergy, are going outside the box to build bridges. This quote from the *Telegraph* story summarizes it: "But outside the portico of a handsome Georgian church stands an anachronistic figure. His white surplice flapping in the wind, vicar Simon Harvey is intent on luring shoppers into his Sunday service."[7] Success for Harvey is gathering one hundred worshippers in his old church.

American Christianity seems like a world away from the staid, old Church of England. This is especially true of California Christianity. The factor that unites these two disparate entities is the secular world outside the church building. Francis Chan went from the hot house of seminary to serve at Cornerstone Community Church in Simi Valley, the technological center of our world. Then he realized there were more people outside who needed to hear the message. He resigned from this rather cushy pastoral position and headed for San Francisco, where secularism meets social experimentation. This sacrificial move is indicative of Chan's sacrificial lifestyle.

Chan has given away more than 90 percent of his income to various ministries and charities. He models sacrificial servant leadership in the most difficult way possible. His heart cry is for sex slaves in foreign countries, a missional outreach that moves Sandals Church in Riverside, California also.

At Bristol City Centre Church servant leadership is part of the church's DNA. When the doors opened lead pastor Mark Detzler expressed his vision: "We believe that God has a wonderful plan and purpose for this ministry. We trust him to lead and guide us as we set out the everlasting truths of his Word and as we bring that truth to bear on those who are his disciples and those who are yet to become disciples."[8]

The English emphasis is on depth, spiritual depth in the pulpit and in the listener. Over the years there has always been skepticism about the more superficial approach of American Christians. However, servant leadership is emerging in the American churches as well. Derwin Gray includes this in the manifesto of Transformation Church: "We are committed, by the Spirit's enabling power, to develop a biblical, servant-hearted community, in which we serve each other through our grace-gifts as we serve in our spheres of influence by being the heart, hands, and feet of Jesus."

---

7. Oborne, "The Return to Religion."

8. Detzler, "Proclaiming Christ in the City Centre." Unpublished circular letter. September 2012.

Emerging Awakening—A Faith Quake

As I write, the leaders of Sanctuary in Fairfield, Connecticut have invited me to give instruction to their core team on the subject of spiritual warfare. After practicing and teaching in this area for more than thirty years, I find the questions from Millennials to be the most challenging ever. They are serious about spiritual living, and they are especially serious about issues of spiritual warfare.

Elevation Church in Charlotte, North Carolina adds a deeper dimension to this discussion. Steven Furtick has taught this exciting group of Christ followers the reality of servant leadership. Not only does the pastoral staff lead the way in generous financial giving, but they also exhibit servant leadership in their concentrated efforts to reach young adults throughout the city. When we first visited Elevation, I was amazed. It started when we drove into the parking lot, and the effusive effort to serve us never stopped. Pastoral staff patiently explained the ministry. Ushers guided us through each aspect of worship, having led us to front row seats. At the end of the evening, they accompanied us out of the worship center and helped us to exit the parking lot. Serving seems to be part of the DNA at Elevation also.

As one of the main teachers of the emerging movement in the United States, Mark Driscoll also formulates the truth that leaders are servants. In his discussion of the first ten years at Mars Hill Church, Driscoll turns to the subject of service. He explains it clearly: "In addition to training and raising up leaders in official church positions such as elder and deacon, we also made it clear that our members were expected to be missionaries and to do the work of the ministry in their daily life and among each other."[9]

From Fake to Real

Without shame, I take this pithy phrase from Justin Kendrick. He has shaped City Church on a rock solid foundation of authenticity. When he launched City Church the focus fell on authenticity. The handout read: "This is not stagnant, distant, traditional religion. It's a living, honest, authentic lifestyle." The phrase, "authentic lifestyle," shouted out in bold, bright yellow print.

Francis Chan agrees with Kendrick. He often speaks of "what the Bible is really saying." Then he goes straight to application and adds the

---

9. Driscoll, "Ten Painful Lessons."

importance of, "really living our lives that way."[10] Chan is hard on tepid, lukewarm Christian living. He sees this as the sworn enemy of authenticity.

At Elevation Church the crowds sometimes blind people to the core of commitment that motivates Steven Furtick and his team. A twelve-point code defines the essence of Elevation, and each point is buttressed by authenticity. It sounds risky when Furtick says, "We are more concerned with the people we are trying to reach than the people we are trying to keep." This raises the hackles of traditional Christians, who want the church to cater to their whims and tantrums. Furtick has no room for soft saints sitting without serving. He heads this discussion with a confrontational phrase, "We need your seat."[11]

Furtick's passion for authenticity extends to the very heart of Elevation's evangelism in the greater Charlotte area. "We are known for what we are for," is the phrase that encapsulates this. Then he explains, "We will speak vision and life over people. We will lift up the salvation of Jesus rather than using our platform to condemn."[12] Furtick and his team will not be dissuaded from the design they believe God has given them. They are truly single-minded in their desire to display an authentic lifestyle to the community at large.

Not unexpectedly, it is Mark Driscoll who develops the concept of authenticity in his teaching ministry. During the first ten years of Mars Hill Church he was forced to evaluate their role in Seattle and beyond. This drove Driscoll to the following conclusion: "I studied the culture in Seattle and worked hard to pray and plan for our church to connect what was going on in the culture to the Bible."[13] This is one of the most effective statements of cross-cultural ministry in modern America that I have ever heard. How do we connect our time-bound culture to the timeless truths of Scripture?

Driscoll goes deep in his explanation of the process. He speaks out against the concept of enculturation that adapts the message to modernity, or postmodernity in this case. He realizes that this has driven most of missiological study and speculation for the past fifty years, and Driscoll dramatically and directly refutes it. He adds: "I didn't seek to make the gospel relevant, but instead to show the relevancy of the gospel to our culture."[14]

10. Wikipedia, s.v. "Francis Chan," http://en.wikipedia.org/wiki/Francis_Chan.
11. www.elevationchurch.org (accessed December 15, 2011).
12. Ibid.
13. Driscoll, "Ten Painful Lessons."
14. Ibid.

Driscoll never cuts corners with the content of the Christian message. He is fearless in proclaiming the "whole council of God." Many twentieth-century professors of missions and of preaching would have challenged this commitment. Some would have called it foolhardy. Driscoll realizes the Millennial generation wants authenticity from the pulpit, just as they want it in their relationships.

The result was astounding. Driscoll sums it up by writing: "This led to an explosion of conversions, as thousands came to Mars Hill, heard the gospel preached in a way that made sense to them, met Jesus, and were baptized."[15] Ironically, this speaks directly to one of the main criticisms of the church, as expressed by Millennials. David Kinnaman discovered that more than 59 percent of Mosaics or Millennials leave so-called evangelical churches, because the church "fails to connect with the world they live in." When pressed for details they stated that the "Bible was not taught clearly or often enough."[16]

Sanctuary in Fairfield, Connecticut is an interesting microcosm of this phenomenon. The founder of Sanctuary was Kevin Butterfield, who has now moved to Melbourne, Australia. During this time the Bible teaching was strong and solid. Under this intense teaching Sanctuary drew Millennials from every corner of lower Connecticut.

Another example is the ministry of Tim Keller at Redeemer Church in New York. The drive of Redeemer is summarized in their vision statement: "To build a great city for all people through a gospel movement that brings personal conversion, community formation, social justice and cultural renewal to New York City and, through it, to the world."[17]

Keller's fame has spread across the world because of his solid commitment to teaching the Scriptures. He is part of a four-person preaching team that shares the multiple services of Redeemer, as they are spread across New York City. Many of the emerging church lead pastors drink deeply from the wisdom of Tim Keller, although he is definitely of an older generation (incidentally, this demonstrates the commitment of the emerging movement to multi-generational mentoring and ministry).

To be fair, I must remind us that authenticity is not the exclusive property of the Millennial generation. This quest for the real has always been part of generational transition, especially during the twentieth century. For

15. Ibid.
16. Kinnaman, "Six Reasons."
17. "Mission Statement," www.redeemer.com (accessed January 15, 2012).

instance, the Jesus People of the 1960s and 1970s pushed older generations to be real. The Jesus People movement was marked by what was known as "restorationist" theology. They sought to replicate the original life of the early Christians. They often viewed traditional churches as apostate, and they adopted a counter-cultural stance toward social institutions. On a personal level, the Jesus movement advocated simple living, even asceticism. Authenticity was the byword of the Jesus People.

Surely, the most succinct statement of authenticity comes form Sandals Church in Riverside, California. Every contact with them comes down to their mission statement: "Real with self, real with God, and real with others." Christ followers are "working toward all God called them to be in Christ."[18] They seek to develop a relationship with God free of hypocrisy. As they reach out to the world around them, they seek to demonstrate this Christian realism in every relationship. Authenticity is the key to Sandals' existence as a church, and this impacts every member of that faith community. Lead Pastor Matt Brown at Sandals sums up the significance of authenticity for Millennial young adults: "The most important thing for those of us here at Sandals is to learn to be real. I believe the biggest barrier to true Christianity is our false fronts."

From Stand Up to Sing for Real

We have already devoted an entire chapter to the worship of the Millennial believers, but this remains as one of the reasons why they exist. They sincerely try to break with the performance mode of traditional worship. For many years, both contemporary and traditional worship have been tied to the formality of standing up and sitting down. Now the Millennials want to meet God in a real way when they worship. They do not come to church for entertainment. They want more.

Performance characterized worship for centuries. When George Friedric Handel introduced "The Messiah," it was a gala performance in England. As they sang "The Hallelujah Chorus," King George III stood to his feet, and people have stood ever since. Orchestras and opera companies of the world often blurred the line between sacred and secular. In Covent Garden (London), the Metropolitan Opera House (New York), or La Scala (Milan) operas dramatized sacred themes, such as "Samson and Delilah."

---

18. "Mission Statement," www.sandalschurch.com.

These became fodder for the entertainment of operagoers. Seldom was there any sense of the sacred.

Modern entertainment is no better. During the twentieth century, American country music caught the religious market. They turned gospel songs and old-fashioned hymns into top-selling hits. This lent an emotional twinge to performance. At the end of the twentieth century, music mogul Bill Gaither transformed southern gospel music into a multi-million dollar business. Again "worship music" was turned into an entertainment medium.

The Mosaics saw all of this and yearned for authenticity in worship. They wanted to move beyond the standing, shouting crowds of their own concerts. Worship for them must be real, not fake.

From the high energy atmosphere of Elevation Church Christ, Brown summarizes the goal. "I want people to experience the fullness of God," he says. Then he explains: "I want them to be reminded of his faithfulness in their lives. I want the Holy Spirit to move in special ways in their and our lives, to speak to them. I want everything that happens to ultimately point us to Jesus and the cross and the resurrected life in him."[19] Notice the passion for authenticity that runs through Chris Brown's vision for worship at Elevation.

Zenzo Matoga reflects the same purpose. At his United Night of Worship he collected thirty worship leaders on one stage, and this "quickly exploded into a fiery worship movement." He follows the fire motif when he adds: "United Night of Worship is igniting spiritual hunger, passion, and united desperation for Jesus and his manifest presence in the educational hub of our nation [Boston] where thousands from across the world converge."[20] Zenzo orchestrates massive worship events so that every participant can come face to face with God.

On a much smaller scale, Mark Detzler strikes the same chord for worship. At Bristol City Centre Church he insists, "We only use songs that have God as their subject and object. There is no room for self-centered worship." It is not about the worshipper. It is totally about God, and this resonates with Mosaics who are fed up with the narcissism of previous generations.

Obviously, this is not as simple as it sounds. There is always the danger of musicians slipping into a performance mentality, just as the danger persists that attendees become consumers and fans. No one walks this tightrope better than Joel Timothy Houston of Hillsong NYC. Professionally, he has scaled the heights and been rewarded as composer and performer

---

19. Chris Brown, email to author, January 26, 2012.
20. Matoga, www.facebook.com (accessed May 2, 2011).

Why the Church is Emerging

of popular songs. Now he co-pastors Hillsong NYC where his main goal is worship, where he has taken authentic worship to the heart of America's biggest city. For Joel this is a tightrope as he balances between the world of entertainment and the world of worship.

Chris Tomlin walks the same tightrope as Joel Timothy Houston. He has been Male Vocalist of the Year and a Dove Award winner with the Gospel Music Association. So, he has tasted the sweet fruit of success in music, but he has also carved out a life of worship leading. He wrote well-known songs, such as "How Great is Our God" and "If Our God is For Us." These are anthems of worship in many Millennial churches, and Chris Tomlin has influenced the Mosaic generation of worship leaders. Although he has won two Grammy awards for his music, he still devotes his energies mainly to the shaping of real life worship for Millennial Christ followers.

One of the most thoughtful worship leaders in the greater New York area is Rebecca Refvik. She lives in suburban Connecticut, and she is co-leader of worship at Black Rock Congregational Church. She has crossed the generational line through an extremely effective mentoring ministry among young worship leaders.

When asked about authenticity in worship, Rebecca responded in depth. She stands solidly against the performance mentality among musicians, just as she combats the spectator mindset among worshippers. For Rebecca, worship is entering into the presence of God, and this excludes the world. "When we connect with God in heartfelt worship, we realize that this life is not about us. It's about the Lord." As if to underline this statement, she adds: "When we are weak, one of the best things we can do is worship God. Worship brings us into God's presence. Where there is deep joy and true pleasure. Worship causes us to take our eyes off of ourselves and meditate on him."[21]

A Millennial worship leader at Black Rock is John Mendez. When I asked him about the atmosphere of worship, he gave some strong answers. "Why are the lights turned down low in the worship center?" I asked. John responded that this was to exclude any visible distractions and help people concentrate on worship. "Why is the music so loud?" I pressed John. He patiently explained that this helps reticent worshippers to join in. If they know no one can hear them they are more ready to sing out loud. It is all about true authenticity in worship.

---

21. Refvig, email to author, January 24, 2012.

Emerging Awakening—A Faith Quake

Justin Kendrick sums up the secret of authentic Millennial worship. In a classic phrase Kendrick claims: "Our praise supersedes our circumstances." True worship propels us out of our daily dilemmas and into the clarity of God's glory. Kendrick adds the reason for this transformation: "Jesus has triumphed over the demons of hell, all my transgressions, and all of my past."[22] True deliverance ministry is linked inextricably to true worship. As people come to God in worship, they experience the liberation God alone can give us. This is authentic worship.

From Missionary to Missional

For many of us, "missionary" conjures up pictures of old-fashioned folks in pith helmets slogging through the rainforest. More recently, some of us have served as missionaries in major cities around the world: Frankfurt, Nairobi, and Beijing, to name a few. But missionary still spells exotic living.

Millennial leaders have coined a new word: "missional." They see mission as a mandate for every Christian, and the mission field is the world next door. Although Millennials make many missionary junkets to needy places in the world, their prime purpose is a missional lifestyle where they live.

One word of caution is appropriate here. During the late twentieth century Baby Boomers began to reach out and involve themselves in the community. They truly wanted to impact their communities for Christ, but the fortress mentality was too strong. There was a temptation to hide in the holy huddle of church life. There was a scare of secularism, as one by one the institutions of our culture banned overt Christian expression. The public schools are a good example of this. So theoretically, the earlier generation was committed to community involvement. However, this good theory did not always turn to fact. As my friend Norman Geisler has put it many times over the years: "The trouble with beautiful theories is that they get mugged by a brutal gang of facts."

The emerging movement started with missional living and worked back to supportive community life. This explains Mark Driscoll's commitment to train the members of Mars Hill as missionaries. He is simply the missiologist, the trainer. The members fan out into the community and become living lights for the gospel. This concept is not new. The Apostle Paul instructed teachers and preachers to "equip people for the work of service" (Eph 4:12). Paul uses a very unusual Greek word for equipping. It is the

22. Kendrick, sermon preached at City Church, January 22, 2012.

Why the Church is Emerging

word for "setting a broken bone," and Paul urges teachers to fully prepare their listeners, so that the listeners can do the work of service.[23]

So the concept is deeply rooted in the reality of the New Testament. Missional living is biblical living. Driscoll warns about imbalance. "As churches grow, they usually gravitate towards two ends of as ministry spectrum. They either focus on taking care of the people in their church, to the exclusion of those outside the church, or they focus on reaching out to people outside their church to the exclusion of those inside the church."[24]

Driscoll's answer is achieving a proper balance. He teaches that both evangelism of the outsiders and edification of the insiders are essential to healthy church growth. He sums it up: "In order to grow as a church, you must focus on both evangelism and taking care of the people in the church with the same passion and focus."[25]

Sandals Church elevates missional living to the vision statement. They aim to produce Christ followers who are "real with others—joining God on mission as loving members of a local church."[26] The entire flavor of this statement is missional. It is no longer trekking across the desert or through the rainforest to reach unreached tribes with the gospel. Missional living is being Christ followers in the communities where we live and work. An example is one financial executive I met at City Church in New Haven. He works in the heart of New York City's financial district. As we exchange our lives with each other I learn that his propelling passion is to live the life of Jesus at the economic center of our country. He is committed completely to missional living.

Missional living has reversed the twentieth-century model of evangelism. In the previous generations it was bringing lost people to church so that they could hear the preacher and come to faith in Jesus. Missional living launches Christ followers into the community. As Elevation Church puts it, these Christ followers "seeks to bring the gospel to the world.... intent on the ultimate purpose of glorifying Christ."[27]

Although Josh Feay is building a Millennial community within the walls of a traditional church, Black Rock Congregational Church, he works in a missional way. He summarizes his vision in these words: "We want to see people develop into mature disciples who are equipped to glorify God

23. Rienecker, *Sprachlicher Schluessel*, 450.
24. Driscoll, "Ten Painful Lessons."
25. Ibid.
26. www.sandalschurch.com (accessed December 15, 2011).
27. www.elevationchurch.org (accessed December 15, 2011).

through membership in his family, ministry in the church, and mission to our community and beyond." Notice the overt reference to the biblical concept of "equipping" people for the work of ministry. This seems to be part and parcel of the emerging revival movement.

Scot McKnight is not a Millennial, but he has the heart of a young person. He defines the missional aspect of Mosaic churches with this phrase: "The foremost concern of praxis is missional. What does this mean? First, the emerging movement becomes missional by participating, with God, in the redemptive work of God in this world." Second, McKnight adds that the emerging movement becomes missional by "participating in the community where God's redemptive work occurs." Think of Sandals Church and their commitment to combat modern forms of slavery at home and abroad. Third, McKnight explains, "becoming missional means participating in the holistic redemptive work of God in this world."[28] From the anti-slavery work of Sandals Church to the community outreach of City Church in New Haven, the Millennial mission is mainly local. It aims to transform the community by the pervasive presence of Christ followers.

In England, evangelism seems even more direct. At Bristol City Centre Church the pastor is an evangelist. Mark Detzler launched evangelistic ministries both in Italy and England for many years. Now he sees the goal as training evangelists who can serve their community by a gracious invitation to live a life of faith. Here we see the principle of life multiplication at work. The pastor multiplies his ministry when he disciples and trains members of the faith community.

When Hillsong Church created its London branch the result was predictable growth. In twelve years the membership exploded to ten thousand. Their website bears witness to a missional mentality: "We meet during the week in small informal groups, known as Connect Groups, we serve our communities together…we do life together."[29] Missional living has replaced the habit of Sunday-only church attendance, and now the church is seen as people not buildings.

From Sanctuary to Space

The first instinct of traditional churches is to "build a building." Recently, designs were drawn to replace a traditional building. I noticed that the

28. McKnight, "Five Streams of the Emerging Church."
29. Oborne, "The Return to Religion."

architect had included a steeple, and I questioned this. Originally, steeples were bell towers, but this church had not had a bell in years. Not a ding or a dong was ever heard. Later, steeples became identification signs of churches. In Roman times they were square towers, and the Gothic revolution turned them into towering spikes reaching high into the sky. Steeples could be seen from all over town. They were a big, brash advertisement announcing, "there's a church under this steeple."

Inside the building was a huge room known as a sanctuary. Pews populated the room, and they all pointed toward the pulpit. The pulpit was big and imposing. Preachers often called it, "the sacred desk." It was described as the most sacred spot in the whole church.

Prominently in American churches there was also an organ. These were often tucked away in an organ loft in Europe. The organ gave sort of a sweetly sacred sound to worship.

Historically, church has always looked like church. This churchy appearance gave comfort to the old, but it turned off the young. They could not relate to this admittedly artificial atmosphere. Numerous studies have demonstrated this, but none is more complete and compelling than David Kinnaman's book, *You Lost Me*. His study started with kids who attended church during their teenage years, probably as part of a family of churchgoers. At age fifteen a large proportion of them abandoned church because they concluded that Christianity did not intersect with their lives. Kinnaman based his book on a cross-section of eight national studies, which interviewed teenagers, young adults, parents, youth pastors, and senior pastors.[30]

As the emerging movement arose, its leaders realized that "churchy" buildings are not particularly welcoming to Millennials. Lead pastors blazed the path by taking emerging worship to their audience. For instance, Justin Kendrick used the familiar rock music venue of Toad's Place in New Haven. It abuts the Yale campus and is linked with all sorts of familiar acts. It was a perfect place to present the first Easter service of City Church.

When they needed a semi-permanent home, Kendrick chose a brand new arts high school, also near the Yale campus. Here there is a purpose-built theater to stage the performance of drama students. This includes state-of-the-art lighting and sound systems. Young adults enter through a fascinating foyer displaying the artistic production of their own generation. Instantly, they feel at home and the "churchy" barrier is broken down.

---

30. Kinnaman, *You Lost Me*.

Emerging Awakening—A Faith Quake

In North Carolina there is a constant search for accommodation at Elevation Church. Steven Furtick has located several of their centers in shopping malls or strip malls. For instance, when an anchor store became available in a suburban strip mall Elevation snatched it up. They fitted it out as an intimate worship center. In the leftover space they made room for the children of young families. Parking was easy, because it was, after all, a mall. The list of stores in the mall displays, alongside a furniture store, the words, "Elevation church." "Elevation" is written large, and church is written smaller.

When we met friends for dinner one evening I scanned the strip mall where the restaurant was located. Sure enough, there was another site for Elevation Church in that mall. Convenience is compelling, but the subtle suggestion is even more important. By locating churches in malls, Elevation emphasizes the missional lifestyle that fuels the fellowship.

On a Sunday morning in Zurich, Switzerland friends drove through the city, past the sophisticated shopping street to an erstwhile industrial area. We entered what appeared to be a former warehouse building and it opened out into a huge auditorium. Seats surrounded the stage, and music was blaring all the while. This is International Christian Fellowship (ICF). Again, it was ideally suited to its purpose. Not one "churchy" trapping trimmed the building. It was the ideal Millennial worship center for a whole new generation of European young people.

When Mark and Cathy Detzler determined they wanted to birth Bristol City Centre Church, they looked for a space that would be suitable. Along the old harbor side in Bristol they found a modern convention hotel. On the street level was a bar with plenty of room. Glass doors opened out onto the street, which made it a welcoming venue for their purposes. It turned out to be a perfect site to launch the ministry of Bristol City Centre Church, because it put the church almost on the street. Remember, Millennials are missional. They are intent on infiltrating their generation with the living message of the living Lord Jesus.

As they seek a more permanent home, there is a durable determination to stay in the city center of Bristol. This enables them to reach both students at the university and also young professional people who are making their home in the apartments of central Bristol. Missional ministry is all about location, and the Millennial generation is determined to live ministry, not just do ministry.

When Hillsong NYC moved to New York, they too sought a suitable spot. They mainly use the Gramercy Theater for their gatherings, because the crowds are so large. In fact, the line stretches around the block as people wait Sundays for the doors to open. It looks like show time on and off Broadway. Notice once again that worship is embedded in the cultural milieu of Millennials. They worship where they live, not in some super-sanctified church building. Even in London this model thrives. Peter Oborne remarks about the anachronistic appearance of a vicar in full regalia standing outside a handsome Georgian church building in London's secular, left-wing area of Islington.

Christ Church in London was founded over lunch at the Strand Palace Hotel. Because they could not afford a church building, they held early services at the New Connaught Rooms in Covent Garden, near the famous opera house. Later they relocated to the Mermaid Theater. Again, church thrives where people live rather than in outdated old Victorian churches that reek of mold and stale incense.

When the Ghanaian pentecostal Christians worship in London, they meet in the ExCel center. This is a massive, new convention center sprawling along the Royal Victoria Docks area of the capital. At one recent event, the Redeemed Church of God, an African Pentecostal church, drew more than forty thousand for one worship event in the ExCel center. Some of the individual African congregations in England top the ten thousand number, which is almost as many as all the Anglican cathedrals combined.

From Doing Church to Being Church

For centuries, theologians have insisted the church is people not buildings. Alas, they seemed to be whistling in the wind. People still spoke of, "going to church." This meant attending Sunday services in a proper church building. As a historian of revival I despaired of ever winning this battle. I assumed that people would always see church as an event rather than a community of faith.

The emerging movement has changed all that. Scot McKnight has grasped the gist of this movement. He summarizes in these words: "The emerging movement's connection to postmodernity may grab attention and garner criticism, but what most characterizes emerging is the stream best called *praxis*—how the faith is lived out. . . . Its distinctive emphases can be seen in its worship, its concern with orthopraxy, and its missional

Emerging Awakening—A Faith Quake

orientation."[31] It is about being the church rather than just doing church, going through the motions of religious ritual and rites.

The legacy of the emerging movement seems to be a radical readjustment of the church from its formal practices, either traditional or contemporary, to a living form of faith. Mark Driscoll speaks of the time when he grasped this matter, and he adds: "This meant making decisions in light of where we were going rather than where we were—and that meant making some hard decisions, such as closing some popular ministries and locations."[32]

For Francis Chan this involved walking away from the thriving ministry at Cornerstone Community Church in Simi Valley. He turned his back on obvious success to follow the missional vision of reaching San Francisco. This sort of orthopraxy is the earmark of the emerging movement. It has revived Christianity as a way of life, not just a list of doctrine. It is about practicing what we preach rather than promoting propositional teaching.

One of the most touching explanations of this practical faith comes from Anglican vicar, Rob Gilson. For fourteen years he was an actor, and then he followed the call into ministry. He serves St. Saviour's Church tucked in behind Harrod's department store in London. Gilson compares the church to "a sanctuary for wild birds." He explains, "People come when they are wounded and need help—hopefully we will build them up, heal them, and help them fly." It is all about praxis for Gilson too.[33]

From Australia we deduce a final illustration of this practical aspect of the emerging movement. Kevin Butterfield not only serves as lead pastor of a Vineyard church in Melbourne. He has also gathered around him a cluster of committed pastors, who, like him, seek true spiritual awakening. When they gather there are many healings and many deliverances, and many are touched by God in a new way.

On reflection, Kevin concludes they are "very hungry people getting what they are asking, seeking, and knocking for." He refers to the teaching of Jesus that people who ask receive, people who seek find, and people who knock find doors opening (Matt. 7:7). Perhaps this is the best description after all of the emerging revival.

---

31. McKnight, "Five Streams of the Emerging Church."
32. Driscoll, "Ten Painful Lessons."
33. Oborne, "The Return to Religion."

6

Facing Forward—Not Backward

EVERY MAJOR REVIVAL MOVEMENT has been forward looking. It has turned away from the past and its failures. Then the revival movement has surged forward to new life and new vitality. It is not without merit that Mark Driscoll calls the emerging revival "Resurgence." It is indeed resurgence of true faith.

The significance of Resurgence is sketched on their website: "Millions of Christians around the world have come to the Resurgence for training. Our motto is 'We serve leaders,' so our whole mission is to help you on the mission God has given you."[1] There are four main anchors to the Resurgence movement. First, they are passionate about a "Gospel-centered theology," which arises from the Reformation in the sixteenth century. Second, they are passionate about "Spirit-filled lives." They believe teaching about the presence and power of the Holy Spirit is needed in every situation. This ties into the "Jesus living" that we have seen in other emerging contexts. It is the Holy Spirit who enables believers to live like Jesus.

Third, the Resurgence makes a great deal of "complementarian relationships." Taking their model from the Trinity as it displays both relationship and also submission. "The Son submits to the Father, and the Spirit does the work made possible by the sacrifice of the Son." This concept of loving, complementarian submission is the model both for faith communities and families.

Fourth, the Resurgence is strong on the matter of missional churches. Their statement is equally strong: "Churches are not clubs, they are families that comprise members who have been adopted by God. . . . This means

---

1. The Resurgence.

that the church doesn't exist for its own sake, it exists to worship God and love all its neighbors in the name of Jesus."[2]

In many ways, Scot McKnight has become the theologian of the emerging movement. For this reason, his prognosis is a bit academic, but extremely helpful: "If I were a prophet, I'd say that it [the emerging church] will influence most of evangelicalism in its chastened epistemology (if it hasn't already), its emphasis on praxis, and its missional orientation. I see the emerging movement like the Jesus and charismatic movements of the 1960s, which undoubtedly have found a place in the quilt of evangelicalism."[3]

From another perspective, Eddie Gibbs and Ryan Bolger draw a similar conclusion to that of Scot McKnight. They approach it from the standpoint of a new view of salvation: "The gospel of the emerging churches is not confined to personal salvation," they conclude. Then they explain: "It is social transformation arising from the presence and permeation of the reign of Christ."[4] This is a helpful explanation of the concept of missional ministry that we encounter at every turn in our study of the emerging churches.

From the frontlines of the emerging movement, Steven Furtick's code fleshes out this concept of missional thinking. It states: "We dress for the wedding—we will continually increase our capacity by structuring for where we want to go, not where we are. We will remain on the edge of our momentum by overreacting to harness strategic momentum initiatives."[5] This forward-looking approach to leadership has distinguished Elevation, even within the circle of the emerging movement. It has kept Elevation ahead of the pack, so to speak, in the dynamic atmosphere of emerging revival in the southeast United States.

Almost as an appendix to David Kinnaman's thoughtful book, *You Lost Me*, he adds insights from key leaders in the emerging church movement. One of the most powerful contributions is penned by Francis Chan. He recalls the mistakes of the previous generation: "We did everything humanly possible to make church 'easy.' We kept the services short and entertaining, discipleship and evangelism optional, and moral standards low." The result

---

2. Ibid.
3. McKnight, "Five Streams of The Emerging Church."
4. Gibbs and Bolger, *Emerging Churches*, 63.
5. "Code of Elevation Church," as attached to Kim Villarreal's email to author, October 12, 2011.

of all this, according to Chan: "We ended up producing nominal Christians whose unchanged lives have deterred others from being interested."[6]

After this dismal description of worship during the past generation, Chan characterizes the Millennial generation as young adults, who "are studying the Bible without missing the obvious." They reject the "shallow methodology" of the past, and they view it as being "incongruent with the Jesus of Scripture." About either our traditional or our contemporary church services Chan writes: "They [Millennials] are bored with Sunday morning productions and long to experience the Holy Spirit." He sounds like Mark Driscoll when he concludes: "This generation sees the potency of a church where pastors equip and shepherd disciple-makers rather than service-attenders."[7] Mark Driscoll explains that growth is an inevitable aspect of the emerging church. He challenges leaders to grow with the community, as leaders must metamorphose to meet the challenge of each new era in their ministry.

As I write these words we have just experienced a day of training with Millennial Christ followers. They pushed and prodded me to take them ever deeper into the subject of spiritual warfare. At the end of the seminar I was exhausted, but they were just catching a second wind. For more than an hour they counseled with our leadership team. They sought spiritual guidance even as they cried out to God for healing in their situations, their families, and their bodies. As we walked to the door, some followed us asking for more.

There is a depth of hunger among the Millennial Christ followers that I have seen in more than fifty years of ministry. It reminds me of the biblical picture of the patriarch Jacob as he wrestled with God at Peniel. As dawn breaks over the valley, Jacob cries out: "I will not let You go unless You bless me" (Gen 32:26). God honors him with a new name—Israel—and it means he has actually struggled with God and prevailed.

This is the mindset of the Millennial believers. They are determined to follow God until he blesses them. They are committed to being filled with the Holy Spirit. They believe God can breathe life back into the dry bones of American Christianity. Although they have never seen a revival first hand, God has given them a vision of what it will look like.

In matters of the emerging church, my trusted mentor is Justin Kendrick. On New Years Day 2012 he hosted a time of worship and vision. Then he finished with this ringing affirmation of God's faithfulness: "We will see

---

6. Kinnaman, *You Lost Me*, 215–16.
7. Ibid.

Emerging Awakening—A Faith Quake

in the next twelve months what people say is impossible in New England."[8] This is most certainly the vision of the emerging church movement. They see God sweeping our land with the greatest revival ever, and they believe that he can and will do it. There is no room for business as usual. No place exists for nominal believers. This is a new day, and it will be matched by a new demonstration of God's power.

Forgetting the Fractures

Millennial young adults have grown up in a world of broken promises, fractured families, and humiliated church leaders. These cracks in the social structure are particularly apparent because of the wall-to-wall coverage of communications media. Each smart phone user packs enough power to link with anybody worldwide, and news spreads faster than the speed of light.

Fractured Families

During the childhood of most Millennials, divorce divided families at an epidemic rate. Furthermore, the churches that opposed divorce in the past now embraced it as inevitable reality. To quote Phyllis Tickle's insightful book, *The Great Emergence*, "But in time divorce came (to the church) anyway, leaving in its wake the inevitable and predictable carnage of family instability and too easy escape from the problems of shard living."[9] Arguably, the victims of this shift are the Millennials, and they know it.

This is personal for Millennials who have experienced the explosion of their family. Justin Kendrick tackled it in an early sermon at City Church. He acknowledged the pain and grief that overwhelms children of divorced families. He went further and recognized the rage that marks relationships, or lack of relationships, between Millennial young adults and their divorced parents.

Then Justin Kendrick challenged his contemporaries to accept God's healing of these intense pains. He led them to the gate of forgiveness and encouraged them to go through to true freedom as they forgive their parents. So deeply does Justin sense this need that he requires young adults to

---

8. Kendrick, sermon, January 1, 2012.
9. Tickle, *The Great Emergence*, 100.

deal with generational bondage before they can accept a leadership position at City Church.

The serious approach of Justin Kendrick is indicative of the spiritual depth visible in the emerging movement. Recently, I was asked to teach a group of Millennial leaders about spiritual warfare. Almost immediately, the stress of separation and divorce surfaced. Patiently, we taught the affected leaders about the true deliverance available through the Lord. After a two-to-three hour session on a Saturday morning, several of the young leaders lingered behind for personal prayer. We prayed for almost every imaginable form of healing, especially healing of generational bondage due to divorce.

While teaching at a major university I was preparing early one morning for class, and a student athlete appeared at the door. She dissolved into tears as she walked across the room to my desk. I asked the open-ended question, "What's happening?" She began, "Last night I had a call from my mom. She and my dad are breaking up. They are getting a divorce." The sobs of that usually confident athlete linger in my mind. For the remaining time before class I counseled and prayed with her. Then I sent her back to the dorm to call her mom and hopefully start a healing process.

Mark Driscoll seldom, if ever, speaks of marriage without challenging Millennials to grow beyond the models of marriage breakdown in their families. Driscoll challenges men to act like men, claiming, "We have an epidemic of adolescence. Men are babies. This is the Peter Pan syndrome." In reality, the emerging churches are challenged by an almost complete lack of model marriages, where husbands and wives walk in the Spirit.

At Black Rock Church in Fairfield, Connecticut my wife and I teach a class on discipling in the family. At first, attendees think this is about their children. Really, we are extending the concept of discipleship to every relationship within the family, including the husband and wife relationship.

Derwin Gray gets it. He writes of Transformation Church: "We are committed, through the Spirit's enabling power, to be a community that invites and seeks out the wounded, the broken-hearted, and the marginalized so that they can be transformed by the Gospel of grace into the image of Jesus joining Him in His mission to transform the world."[10]

---

10. Gray, email to author, October 5, 2011.

Emerging Awakening—A Faith Quake

Shattered Churches

A second area of healing is the dismal record of clergy abuse and failure. During the late twentieth century, television preachers failed with monotonous regularity. Mega-church pastors became laughing stocks. Venerable institutions, like the Catholic Church, were shaken to the root by accusations of priestly abuse and molestation. The emerging movement tries to distance itself from these blots on the body of Christ. By using different forms, different leaders, and even different venues, the emerging movement attempts to eradicate the painful memories of religious failure.

When Elevation emerged in the Charlotte, North Carolina area it was welcomed by the young and feared by the old, and the almost old. Traditional churches have invested millions of dollars in building massive structures strung along the main arteries of that southern city. These huge, would-be cathedrals compelled them to constant giving and unending upkeep. Gigantic staffs of pastors and support personnel were engaged to keep the machine oiled. Elevation first met in a local high school. Then it spread to renovated buildings in strip malls that had gone dark. The whole feel of Elevation worship was foreign, even frightening, to the Baby Boomers. In the meantime their children, the Mosaics or Millennials, broke down the doors to worship at Elevation.

As part of the Southern Baptist Convention, Elevation had achieved another coup. It had sidestepped the seething strife between conservatives and moderates in that massive denomination. Conservatives championed the historical evangelical faith. Moderates moved into a more conciliatory posture toward doctrinal issues. It looked as if the great ship of Southern Baptists might scuttle on the rocks of this controversy.

Elevation led the way to a new approach for a new generation. They reached out to draw Millennial young adults into a warm, personal relationship with Jesus Christ. On the west coast, Sandals Church sought the same kind of role in the Southern Baptist Convention. Lead pastor Matt Brown turned to Rick Warren at Saddleback Church for advice and guidance. Together they developed the emerging model of Sandals, and it has provided a warm worship experience for Millennial adults in the university town of Riverside, California.

As if on cue, in nearby Orange County the Baby Boomer monument, Crystal Cathedral, has fallen on hard times. It made headlines when the aging senior minister fired his young son. A short while later the glass church was back in the headlines, as it declared bankruptcy and fell into the

Facing Forward—Not Backward

hands of receivers. In many ways it was a microcosm of the shift from Baby Boomers to Millennials, from historic evangelicalism to emerging church.

When Bristol City Centre Church was born in Bristol, England it broke away from a traditional, evangelical preaching center—Kensington Baptist Church. In a stroke of wisdom, the Kensington elders endorsed Bristol City Centre Church and encouraged Mark and Cathy Detzler to open a site in Bristol city center. This is, in many ways, the best way for generations to share in the change process of emerging Christianity.

Revivals Remembered

Revival is the reason for this book. Early in my career I carved out a role as a historian of revival, and my entire ministry has been devoted to preaching in the midst of revival movements, writing about them, and teaching principles derived from them. Four revival movements sketch my pathway. The post-depression revival in industrial America brought our family to faith. During my early missionary career, older brothers mentored me in preaching as part of a revival movement in the Baden district of Germany. As lead pastor in Bristol, England, we experienced a brief, somewhat rocky revival. Finally, my wife and I were privileged to be part of a revival movement in the Fangcheng Church in China.[11]

Gibbs and Bolger broach the subject of revival in the emerging church. Gibbs and Bolger write to some degree from a British perspective. They see the emerging church as reviving the existent structure, such as the Anglican Church. Typical of British conservatism, they conclude: "Rebuilding will come, but it cannot be rushed." They see revival more as evolution than as revolution.[12]

It is good to pause and remind ourselves that the Millennial generation has never seen a revival like the charismatic renewal of the 1960s and the Jesus People, who emerged then also. Never has the Millennial generation seen a passionate nationwide movement like the Welsh revival of the early twentieth century. Phyllis Tickler touches on this in *The Great Emergence*. She quotes Donald Miller from the University of Southern California. He holds the Firestone Professorship of Religion. Miller notes that these "new paradigm churches" are in the process of creating an entirely "new genre of worship music, restructuring the organizational character of institutional

---

11. Aikman, *Jesus in Beijing*, 74–81.
12. Gibbs and Bolder, *Emerging Churches*, 27–28.

religion, and democratizing access to the sacred by radicalizing the Protestant principle of the priesthood of believers.[13]

When it comes to models for missional ministry, leaders of the emerging churches often return to revival voices of the past. I asked Justin Kendrick who most influenced his approach to revival, and he mentioned John Wesley and Charles Haddon Spurgeon. Then he added Reinhard Bonnke, a charismatic evangelist known for his expansive ministry in Africa. It is estimated that more than fifty-two million have professed faith in Christ because of Bonnke's preaching during the past forty years. This is the level of revival Kendrick seeks for New England as he launches City Church in New Haven.

Another connection to historical renewal is Mark Driscoll's depth of commitment to the teaching and work of Martin Luther. He adds, "Martin Luther is a personal hero of mine. We need to be Christ-centered, not just cause-centered."[14] So caught up in reformational thinking is Driscoll that he reads deeply in the writings of people like John Calvin, Jonathan Edwards, and Charles Haddon Spurgeon. Driscoll sees a historical link between these generational power preachers as they carried forth the truths of the Protestant Reformation.

Often Driscoll hearkens back to the *sola scriptura* (Scripture only) stance of the Reformers. He sees this as the bedrock of ministry at Mars Hill and in the wider circle of the Resurgence. In fact, Driscoll refers people to the "Five Solas" of the Reformation. They are: sola scriptura (Scripture alone), sola fide (faith alone), sola gratia (grace alone), solus Christus (Christ alone), and soli Deo gloria (God's glory alone).[15] As he leads the Resurgence, one has the impression that Driscoll will be content with nothing less than a new Reformation. He chooses the Reformation as his model for revival because of the solid theological basis it developed.

When I asked Justin Pardee about the spiritual roots of Sandals Church in Riverside, California he pointed to Rick Warren at Saddleback Church. Sandals' lead pastor Matt Brown was mentored by Rick Warren, and this infused him with a passion for revival and renewal. The subsequent growth of Sandals has reproduced in the Millennial generation what Rick Warren saw in the Baby Boomer generation. The purpose that drives Sandals is their often-repeated mantra: "Real with self, real with

---

13. Tickle, *Great Emergence*, 155.

14. Driscoll, "Four Points."

15. http://driscollwatch.wordpress.com/2010/09/08/online-content-review-sola-scriptura (accessed September 25, 2012).

God, real with others."[16] The revival movement among Millennials is first and foremost an authentic movement.

Derwin Gray pointed to Bill Hybels at Willow Creek Community Church as his model for ministry. Then he added that Ken Boa is his model for apologetics. Ken Boa and Robert Brown wrote the hugely successful text on apologetics, *Faith Has Its Reasons*. Derwin Gray sees his goal as reaching an entire generation with the gospel. The aggression he demonstrated as a pro football linebacker has now been channeled into the task of hunting down people for Christ.

Derwin Gray also made an extremely wise geographical choice when he launched Transformation Church. He positioned it on one of the fastest growing edges of the metropolitan Charlotte area, also known as Metrolina. By reaching the explosive communities of South Carolina, Gray has caught a wave of people who are particularly receptive to the Christian message.

The International Christian Fellowship in Zurich, Switzerland is heir to almost a half-century of revival movement. In the early 1960s George Verwer moved to Europe to launch Operation Mobilization. The result was a revival movement among young adults, a movement that emphasized deep, complete commitment to the things of God.

Out of Operation Mobilization came a young couple, Heinz and Annelies Strupler. They sensed a call of God to concentrate their efforts on their hometown of Zurich. For more than forty years they have disciple young adults and planted churches in the Zurich area. It was their vision that birthed International Christian Fellowship. Immediately, they turned the leadership over to key young pastors like Hansjörg Stadelmann. This set ICF on a course to capture the Mosaic population of Zurich and beyond. So the face is young, but the virility of ICF has deep roots in the true revival movement of Operation Mobilization during the second half of the twentieth century.

Turning from Me to God

Millennials are reacting to the market-driven model of church. When they speak about their parents' generation and their parents' churches, they talk about a consumer concept of church. Millennials remember church as a place where the pastor is a CEO at the head of a marketing organization. Everything from children's ministries to worship ministries are seen as

16. Pardee, email to author, January 19, 2012.

means to an end. The end is landing the sale, winning another member for the mega-church congregation. Millennials may have a jaded view of this phenomenon, but they are still seeking to distance themselves from it.

Gibbs and Bolger cut to the core of the issue when they write: "Churches that adopt a marketing approach treat their visitors as customers, numbers, and potential converts instead of simply as people. A culture of self-interested exchange permeates the life of the customer-oriented churches, where the 'customer's' financial support is solicited in exchange for spiritual services rendered."[17] In reality, Christian discipleship is "worldview modification." Douglas Potter and I explore this in our book, *Cross-Cultural Apologetics*. Millennials view their parents as products of a consumer-centered worldview. Consequently, church became for them yet another consumer choice. This involved "church hopping," as they sought the best bargain. Again, this is a jaded view, which arises because of the gap between Baby Boomers and their Millennial offspring. However, it does shape the approach of emerging churches.

Elevation's code expresses this God-centered approach in a concise yet explicit way. The final item in the code declares: "We will not take this for granted—what we are experiencing is not normal. This is the highest calling, and we will remain grateful for God's hand of favor."[18] In fact, throughout the twelve points of the code, there is frequent reference to God's work in and through the life of Elevation Church. It seems to me that they have a remarkable sense of dependence on God.

If this is true of Elevation, it is also the case with Transformation Church. Every item in their values statement is prefaced with the phrase: "through the Spirit's enabling." Here again repetition is used to reinforce the concept of dependence on God. They specifically reject the consumer mentality, when they assert: "We are committed, by the Spirit's enabling power, to value people more than what they can produce. We will not prostitute people over and against their spiritual health and transformation."

The director of worship at Transformation is Angela Lear. She wholeheartedly supports this God-centered worldview, when she responds to the question: "What do you want people to experience about God as you lead them in worship?" Angela answers: "Our hope is that we will sing songs and play music in such a way that people will experience and see God as high

---

17. Gibbs and Bolger, *Emerging Churches*, 137.

18. "Code of Elevation Church," as attached to Kim Villarreal's email to author, October 12, 2011.

and lofty, the King of Kings and Lord of Lords, who is worthy of all praise; and in doing so, they will recognize that very same God loves them with a passionate and unending love."[19] After a life of worship leading, this is the first time I have encountered such a God-centered approach from the worship director. Usually, rehearsal is about the right notes and the right beat. Angela's approach is about the right heart. She has totally come into agreement with Derwin Gray's pledge not to prostitute people, not to use them as objects.

Scot McKnight writes out of the experience of the emerging movement, and as a theologian he helps formulate the approach. McKnight calls this "holistic" ministry. They take as their model Jesus-living. Jesus "picked the marginalized up from the floor and put them back in their seats at the table; he attracted harlots and tax collectors; he made the lame walk and opened the ears of the deaf. He cared, in other words, not just for lost souls, but also about whole persons and whole societies."[20]

For many years I did not understand "holistic ministry." It took our brothers and sisters in China to teach me. Le Anna was our assistant and translator, who became a daughter to us. She explained that the vast majority of people now coming to Christ in China do so through healing. They come to the church for healing, and when God restores them they become believers. Each Sunday as we served in apartment-churches, we had ample opportunity to engage in and learn more about such holistic ministry.

Justin Kendrick reframed this discussion about hearing God when he taught City Church. He carefully excluded hackneyed approaches. It is not about the "fleece method," as Gideon put out a fleece and dared God to make it wet or make it dry just to satisfy his doubts. Nor was this about the door method that sees any open door as God's guidance. After all, when Jonah fled from the Lord, he found a ship waiting to take him in the opposite direction.

Kendrick also discards the "other people method," where we rely on other people to tell us what to do (one of the most successful pastors in the twentieth century gave me the worst advice about my own pastoral ministry). Likewise, Kendrick rejects the "Bible dipping" approach, whereby we let the Bible fall open and take the first verse we see as God's guidance.

Kendrick asserts that in reality we are "hard-wired to hear God." Notice that he emphasizes this God-centered, God-focused approach again. Then he expands it: "You are already hard-wired to hear God and walk with the Holy Spirit." The believer who walks in the Spirit of God will always

19. Lear, email to author, October 27, 2011.
20. McKnight, "Five Streams of the Emerging Church."

Emerging Awakening—A Faith Quake

have the guidance he or she needs. Notice how Kendrick emphasizes the importance of living in the Spirit and listening to the Spirit. He ends with a rather memorable sentence: "God directs you as you act in full expectation that God will direct you."[21]

Kendrick seems a world away from Peter Oborne, the *Telegraph* journalist. In reality, Oborne is describing a similar emerging movement in London. One of his informants is Simon Harvey, the second career vicar of St. Mary's in Upper Street, in the Islington section of London. Simon believes there is still a yearning for faith among the Millennial generation in London. He too refers to the consumer mentality of the late twentieth century when he says: "There have been many wonderful things about the last half-century, but it is impossible to deny that it has been an era of materialism and selfishness."[22] It is the experience of Simon Harvey at St. Mary's that once people come through the door they are open to friendship and welcome. Soon people settle into the community and the issues of faith follow from that. Here again the emphasis falls on holistic ministry in the secular city.

The link between holistic ministry and God-centered ministry must be made. If God is the creator, he has a vested interest in each of his creatures. When we approach them holistically, we affirm the fact that they are not disembodied spirits like angels, they are real people, with real needs, living in a very real world.

From Suburbs to Cities

At the end of the final section we referred to Peter Oborne's excellent report on religion in postmodern London. It is indicative of the emphasis on urban ministry among Millennials. They have grown up in the picket-fenced suburbs and have discovered that behind the façade is frustration. Now they turn back to the cities to exercise their healing ministry. Oborne summarizes this when he writes: "Church attendances, in free-fall for so long, have started to rise again, particularly in Britain's capital city."[23]

As he prepared to launch City Church Justin Kendrick made it abundantly plain: his object was to reach New Haven, Connecticut with the Christian message couched in Christian love. In his own words, Kendrick said: "We started City Church to see actual change in the city of New

---

21. Kendrick, sermon, January 22, 2012.
22. Oborne, "The Return to Religion."
23. Ibid.

Facing Forward—Not Backward

Haven."[24] This passion for the city is bigger than evangelism. It is more than saving souls; it also bigger than building a church and filling seats. Kendrick will be content with nothing less than permeating the culture of the community with credible Christian witness.

Kendrick fleshes out his vision with three bold statements. He wants to see businesses expand in New Haven, so jobs are available. Second, he wants to see safer streets. Ironically, the hometown of Yale University is also one of the most murderous towns in the nation. Third, Kendrick aims for honest government. It is very likely that members of City Church will ultimately find their way into the chambers of New Haven government. This is missional thinking at its very best.

This commitment to penetrate the cities with the Christian message is described in very earthy language. Chris Matthews of Linden Church in Swansea, Wales puts it this way: "We created a service, Extreme, at the café for the new Christians. . . A church ought to look like a pub, bright and inviting."[25]

Reaching the city is job number one for Elevation Church also. In their code they express this as a priority: "We will not cater to personal preference in our mission to reach this city." Consequently, they continue to open worship venues in strip malls around the city of Charlotte, and each one is soon filled with an emerging crowd of seeking young adults.

Across the country in Seattle, Mark Driscoll has become the model for many of these ministries. He takes this mentoring responsibility very seriously, as one can see in the explosive growth of the Resurgence. Driscoll regards every member of his congregation as a missionary. Their task is to reach the community with the Christian message. Driscoll's phrase says it all: "The church is sent and it is sending."[26] This concept is based on the biblical principle of a pastor training his people do to works of service (Eph 4:12–16). In effect, the pastor becomes a missiologist, strategizing to reach the community at large. Driscoll even uses that technical term "missiologist" when he describes his role as lead pastor at Mars Hill Church.

Driscoll always takes his people back to the Bible. In finding a model of missional ministry he refers to the explosive growth of the gospel at the day of Pentecost (Acts 2:1–48). Here he sketches the fact that 120 disciples dared to be missionaries, and the end result was the baptism of

---

24. Kendrick, sermon, January 22, 2011.
25. Gibbs and Bolger, *Emerging Churches*, 121.
26. Driscoll, "Four Points."

three thousand believers in one day. Peter preached and people responded. Driscoll draws a lesson from this: "Had he [Peter] not done that, we'd be pagans. It's never about comfort; it's always about Jesus."[27]

In the city of Bristol, England Mark and Cathy Detzler have birthed Bristol City Center Church. It took more than a year to build their core group, and they relied on the mother church, Kensington Baptist Church, for support during this team-building time. At the end of the year they launched the ministry in the Premier Inn coffee shop, a bright, airy room with glass doors on two sides. Mark Detzler explains: "We found that we were able to throw open the double doors and allow passersby to stand on the street and be impacted by the singing and the preaching."[28] This creates an open opinion among the Millennials who live nearby. They can take a good long look before stepping into the room for the first time. The non-threatening approach to outreach is a crucial element of emerging church success.

When Heinz and Annelies Strupler started International Christian Fellowship (ICF) in Zurich, they embedded it in the heart of the city. Zurich is known for its chic European style, but it is also home to thousands of young adults. Many of these are away from home for the first time. As uprooted people, they are especially receptive to the warmth of ICF. Added to that, the worship is a popular blend of English and German, a pattern familiar from the pop scene. The preaching, however, is always given in Swiss German, which is the heart language of young adults now living in the city.

As a result of this remarkable blend of the hip and the familiar, young adults in Zurich flock to ICF. Each weekend more than two thousand attend eight different services. Deep in the heart of Zurich there is a credible, Christian presence that bypasses the age-old traditions of the Reformation and reaches out for the hands and hearts of young Swiss and international residents of the city.

Real Hope for Real Needs

Throughout our study we have seen that the emerging movement is missional. Scot McKnight lists three ways in which the emerging churches are missional, "by participating, with God, in the redemptive work of God in this world." This gives new and deeper meaning to what the Apostle Paul

27. Ibid., "Ten Painful Lessons."

28. Mark Detzler, "Preaching Christ in the City Centre." Unpublished newsletter. September 2012.

called "the ministry of reconciliation" (2 Cor 5:18). Second, the emerging church takes an active role by "participating in the community where God's redemptive work occurs." The church in its community life gives credibility to the gospel, and the emerging church has broadened the meaning of community ministry significantly. Third, missional refers to the holistic work done by the emerging churches in the world at large. This is seen as taking steps toward the ultimate healing that is foretold and foreshadowed in the book of Romans (Rom 8:18–27).[29]

Eddie Gibbs and Ryan Bolger make a great deal out of the missional aspect of the emerging churches. They quote a seminal statement by Anna Dodridge from Bournemouth in the United Kingdom. She claims: "Our commitment is to be missionary at all times. Everything we do in our lifestyle, in what we say, in how we treat people, that's all our witness. It's all mission."[30]

This missional concept goes deep. Steve Collins of London explains: "Secular space is a bubble in the surrounding water. It is a place where God has been excluded. I don't believe in 'secular.' It shouldn't exist."[31] No sphere of life is excluded form the missional activity of the emerging movement.

Gibbs and Bolger summarize this rather deep concept when they conclude: "We are commanded by Christ as his followers to live incarnationally, to overcome boundaries, to express the God-life, and to recognize where God is at work in every realm."[32]

Mark Driscoll returns often to the theme of missional living, as he sees every Christian as a missionary and the pastor as a missiologist preparing the Christian for his or her task. In local situations Driscoll explains this, but in general he is trying to recapture the biblical concept of Christians permeating society with the life-giving message of the gospel. This is a modern and very relevant version of the Reformation doctrine of the priesthood of all believers.

For centuries we in the academic world have wrestled with the biblical teaching about the priesthood of believers (1 Pet 2:5). It has come into focus more clearly as leaders of the emerging movement have created the concept of missional living. At Sandals Church in Riverside, California lead pastor Matt Brown has built a ministry designed to expose and exterminate modern-day slavery, human trafficking. He explains that this is modern slavery

---

29. McKnight, "Five Streams of the Emerging Church."
30. Gibbs and Bolger, *Emerging Churches*, 58.
31. Ibid., 67.
32. Ibid., 75.

that begins with the promise of a job in America and becomes forced labor or debt servitude. Few would know about this horrendous abuse of newly arrived immigrants had it not been for the exposure given by Matt Brown.

In Bristol, England Mark Detzler pairs pastoral ministry at Bristol City Centre Church with a teaching appointment in a city college. As their newsletter explains it, "He [Mark] continues to teach English to Muslims from Somalia and other un-reached people groups. The role of teacher means that he is often able to share the gospel and steer the discussion towards spiritual matters." One Pakistani Muslim man was so intrigued that he asked for one of Mark's sermons.

Separately, an Iranian group has been developed to provide an introductory class about Christianity, the Alpha Study. Taught in Farsi, Mark uses talks prepared by an Iranian pastor. In recent years, several Iranians have been baptized following their decision to become Christ followers. Here too the church becomes a welcome source of encouragement to newly arrived immigrants in the United Kingdom.

Missional living not only impacts immigrant populations. It also aids the disenfranchised in America. Early on in the ministry of City Church, Justin Kendrick held a summer festival on the Green in New Haven, Connecticut. He called it "I love New Haven." More than 1,400 flocked to the event. There were all sorts of entertainment for children and adults, and there was an abundance of food. As a sound backdrop for the day, Christian bands belted out music over loudspeakers. At crucial breaks Justin and members of his band shared a gospel witness. This one-day event put City Church on the map in New Haven, but it also established the missional ministry that continues to characterize the faith community.

After "I love New Haven," members of the City Church community donated 1,400 hours of community service. They had committed beforehand to spend one hour in community service for each attendee at the event on the Green. There is a continuing impact of missional ministry throughout New Haven, where the "town and gown" split is so blatant. On one hand, New Haven hosts a premier academic community—Yale University. On the other hand, it is one of the most needy cities in New England. City Church is committed to not only bridging the gap, but it is bent also on building an entirely new community of life in New Haven.

When I asked Hansjörg Stadelmann about the missional aspect of International Christian Fellowship (ICF) in Zurich, Switzerland, he was somewhat perplexed. Missional living is so ingrained in the DNA of his ministry that it is hard to see. He cited four core values of ICF with four German words (translation mine):

- *Multiplikativ*—"multiplying," as the love of Jesus jumps from one person to another.
- *Übernatürlich*—"supernatural," because everything is possible with God.
- *Stadtrelevant*—"relevant to the city," because God loves all people.
- *Vernetzt*—"connected," because relationships make us strong.

Notice how Hansjörg blends missional thinking with the very essence of ICF in Zurich. This seems to be a pattern of emerging churches. At first, their missional activity is somewhat awkward and uncomfortable. Eventually, however, it becomes so natural that it cannot be factored out of the fabric of church life.

Transformation Church in suburban South Carolina is relatively new, so there is an explicit effort to incorporate missional activity into the life and work of the church. Derwin Gray casts the vision in this way: "The vision of Transformation Church is to be a multi-ethnic, multi-generational, mission-shaped community that loves God completely, ourselves correctly, and our neighbors compassionately."[33]

This succinct statement is designed to imbed the vision in the hearts of Transformation members. It is also formulated simply so each person can understand it. Derwin Gray, an African-American is married to Vicki, who is white. Together they have two beautiful, teenaged children. As a family they model the vision for their church, and thus they give vibrancy and vitality to their discipleship ministry. The worship team is likewise multi-ethnic, and this further strengthens the vision of Transformation Church. From a missional standpoint, the multi-ethnic aspect of Transformation Church opens doors across the community. It creates a welcoming atmosphere, where visitors can catch the vision in an unthreatening environment.

Doing Church in a New Way

The emerging churches have carved out a whole new approach to church. Phyllis Tickle admits to being baffled by the emerging church movement.

33. Gray, email to author, October 5, 2011.

Emerging Awakening—A Faith Quake

She writes: "There is simply no grand framing story or even unanimity of opinion yet about when precisely it was that this new thing—this new, emerging way of being Christian in an emerging new world—became so clearly distinct from what had been as to be worthy of a name of its own."[34]

While we cannot define exactly what the emerging church means, we can make some conclusions about its nature. Perhaps the most significant is its voyage into new theological waters. First, there is a new view of what exactly it means to be human, what the life as a creature of God in this postmodern world looks like. It is obvious the emerging movement sees each of us as part of the vast view of God's creation, and as such each person is owed the opportunity to hear gospel news.

Second, there is a growing distrust of the received corpus of Christian theology. In the post-Constantinian Christian church theology was infused with Aristotelian philosophy and shaped by that infusion. Salvation shifted from the experience of living out the kingdom of God on earth to "a ticket for a transplantation into a paradisial hereafter" or heaven.[35]

It seems as if the emerging movement is trying to refocus our attention on this world, as it moves us to be intentional about our presence in the cities of the world. We are emissaries of God's heavenly kingdom living and serving in a broken and alienated world. Our aim is to infuse real life, not only into the Christian church, but also into each member of that church. We are called to be missionaries in our world for God's sake.

So we shall turn in our final chapter to the questions that ignited this investigation: Is the emerging church a true revival movement? Is it succeeding in its aim to enliven traditional Christian concepts? Can it endure, or is it only a generational blip on the radar of history?

---

34. Tickle, *The Great Emergence*, 160–61.
35. Ibid.

7

Emerging Revival—Fact or Fantasy?

AT THE OUTSET OF our study we noticed the characteristics of revival in its historical manifestation. It now becomes the duty of this project to overlay the phenomenon of the emerging church with these five criteria of revival. In this concluding chapter we shall attempt to draw connections between recognized revivals of the past and the present emerging movement of God's grace. In each case we shall use examples of the emerging movement to demonstrate the connection.

Prayer becomes Passion

As revival broke out among the house church movement in China, it became clear that this was primarily a prayer movement. The Weepers, for instance were known for their fervency. Centered in the province of Henan, these believers literally cried out to God. The sound of their sobbing haunts me daily.[1]

When Justin Kendrick called together City Church in New Haven, prayer was priority number one. He turned his band into a band of prayer partners, and they became the basis for the emerging church plant. Before any other structure existed he formed a corps of committed prayer counselors. For Justin prayer is part of the missional community, as they place before God each day friends without Jesus. At a Christmas service in New Haven, Justin reminded the crowd: "Our prayer team prays for every request. We are praying for miracles."

Another example of prayer in revival was the Welsh Revival of 1904–1905. Evan Roberts is regarded as the revival leader, but he seldom

---

1. Aikman, *Jesus in Beijing*, 86–87.

preached. His main ministry was public prayer. As he prayed, people fell prostrate before God calling out for mercy. Evan Roberts pled with God for the baptism of the Holy Spirit to sweep across Wales, and it did. The Welsh revival impacted the world. Evan Roberts disappeared after the revival and ultimately died in 1951. His brief prayer ministry was as energetic as it was enigmatic. From 1905 until his death in 1951 Roberts was a recluse, living in the Midlands of England.

Kevin Butterfield got a grip on this aspect of prayer while still in the United States. He became committed to cry out for the baptism of the Spirit, and the Holy Spirit fell in power on him. After moving to Melbourne he produced a prayer ministry called, "Fire Starters." Butterfield described them on his Facebook page as, "very hungry people getting what they are asking and seeking and knocking for."

During the 1980s revival touched Kensington Baptist Church in Bristol, England. It was a Sunday evening when the fire of the Holy Spirit fell on the old church, and I had the privilege of being lead pastor. Powerful prayer and repentance of sin sobered the believers. Until late at night I sat and prayed with penitent people. The primary point of this brief awakening was prayer. An elderly brother who had experienced the Welsh revival of 1904–1905 guided me through this experience, as did Martyn Lloyd-Jones, my mentor. Lloyd-Jones was a charismatic preacher who loved to demonstrate the gifts of the Spirit.

One of my ministry outlets is being part of Sanctuary, a Millennial movement in Fairfield, Connecticut. John Mendez is their worship leader, and he is a man obsessed with prayer. He says: "Whatever happens is because of God. I pray in the midst of leading worship that God will change lives."

Prayer propels the revival among emerging churches, especially in New England. At the heart of the New England prayer movement is a missionary from Malawi: Zenzo Matoga. God has sent him to New England to nurture and grow a movement of prayer, and this demonstrates again the reality of revival among the emerging churches.

The emerging movement is indeed propelled by prayer. It meets this criterion of revival and resembles renewals of the past. Ironically, the ten most secular states in the United States include all six New England states. It is for this reason that City Church has come to call a new generation to revival and prayer. This is as refreshing as a breeze blowing new life into the Millennial generation.

Revival Leaders Appear

Revival leaders mark every revival movement, and very often they are the most unlikely of all. In the past, God snatched selected men from the malaise of humdrum religion and fired them for revival.

Justin Kendrick is one of the brightest young leaders in the emerging movement. In 2011, after several years of travel with his band, Out of Hiding, he started City Church in New Haven, Connecticut. Within a few months he developed the face of ministry in a brand new, ideally suited school theater auditorium.

After juggling travel and pastoral ministries, Justin came to the conclusion that City Church demanded more concentration. In a powerful presentation he revealed the depth of organizational structure of the church, naming the first two elders, himself, and a close associate. Then he underlined the commitment by stating: "I will travel less so that City Church can grow."[2] He had made a costly commitment to demonstrate his devotion to the church.

It sounded much like the experience of Dwight L. Moody as revival swept America in the late 1800s. In 1871 the Great Chicago Fire destroyed 3.3 square miles of the city and killed hundreds. This triggered Moody to make a crucial decision. He eliminated all of his commitments to the Y.M.C.A. and to other organizations so that he could concentrate on preaching.

Revival requires exclusive commitment. This is also true of Derwin Gray at Transformation Church in South Carolina. He had gained fame as a professional football player, but preaching was God's call for his life. So, he described his dedication in this sentence: "Ministry excellence is worship!"[3]

Derwin Gray's story is reminiscent of Billy Sunday, the great evangelist of the early twentieth century. Billy Sunday gained fame as a professional baseball player in Chicago, but the call to preach eclipsed his sports career. He traveled far and wide preaching, and in doing so he ignited the Midwestern revival of the mid-twentieth century.

A third example of revival leadership in the emerging movement is Steven Furtick at Elevation Church in Charlotte, North Carolina. The code that describes ministry at Elevation puts it directly: "Elevation is built on the vision God gave Pastor Steven. We aggressively defend our unity and

---

2. Kendrick, sermon, January 22, 2012.
3. Gray, email to author, October 5, 2011.

that vision."[4] This commitment also reminds us of previous revival movements. Charles Haddon Spurgeon was exemplary in his dedication to the ministry of preaching. He worked nonstop in preparing sermons that have served as models for successive generations. Thousands heard Spurgeon's sermons, and many more read them in the daily newspaper. He became known as the "Prince of Preachers." His devotion to the declaration of the gospel took a toll on his health, and he died at the relatively young age of fifty-eight.

Anointed leaders are a key element in any revival movement. It is my happy discovery that the emerging movement has many revival leaders. Perhaps the best known in the United States is Mark Driscoll. He has developed a coalition of committed preachers, both young and old. It is called the Resurgence, and revival is the stated goal of this movement.

Worship Awakens

Revival always starts people singing. It goes beyond the frozen forms of the past and opens new channels of praise. Matt Richey at Sandals Church in Riverside, California pens one of the best summaries of emerging worship. "Because I love music so much, I am constantly aware that our musical offering to God should be our best."[5] Notice this emphasis on excellence in worship. Then Matt adds: "It has been great to see the ministry grow in number and in excellence, and I look forward to seeing where God takes us as we explore what it means to be real in our music." Notice here the blending of worship and authenticity, which is a key element in the emerging revival.

It reminds me as a historian of the Wesleyan revival in England. Charles Wesley carved out a new course of worship in his estimated six thousand hymns. Each hymn became a heart expression of passion for God, such as "O, For a Thousand Tongues to Sing My Great Redeemer's Praise." This is a prime example of the desire of every revived soul to sing God's praise at the top of her lungs. True revival is carried forward on the wings of song.

Another example of emerging worship leaders is Zenzo Matoga. His very language sizzles with revival. "United Night of Worship is a worship movement where thousands of people from Boston, New England, and across the world gather in desperation to pursue the one, true and living

---

4. "Code of Elevation Church," as attached to Kim Villarreal's email to author, October 12, 2011.

5. www.sandalschurch.com

God, Jesus Christ."[6] The history of this movement goes back to 2007, when Zenzo Geoffrey (his Western name) came as a missionary from Malawi, Africa. Zenzo reports: "A gathering that started with over thirty leaders united on one stage across cultural, denominational, and social lines, has quickly exploded into a fiery worship movement . . . igniting spiritual hunger, passion, and united desperation for Jesus."[7] There is no doubt about this movement; it is the leading edge of revival among emerging churches in New England. Zenzo describes it as "re-digging the wells of revival."

It is very much like the Welsh revival of 1904–1905. It too was a singing revival. Elements of that awakening still linger in great hymns such as, "Guide me, O Thou Great Jehovah." In the late 1970s, one convert of the Welsh revival was Miss Jones of Bournemouth, England. She prayed in my hearing: "O Lord, you know that I have seen revival sweep in like the ocean waves. The tide of revival seems to be out now, but I know the ocean is not empty."

This perpetual hope and prayer for revival characterizes the emerging church movement. As I have spoken with their leaders and met them online and in person, I have discovered there is a heart hunger to see God's touch of revival in their lives, their churches, and above all their cities.

The Lost and the Least

True revival is inextricably connected to evangelism. Revival comes when Christ followers are touched by God and ignited in their passion. Immediately, they reach out to the lost, the lonely, and the least among us. "We are committed, through the Spirit's enabling power, to be a community that invites and seeks out the wounded, the broken-hearted, and marginalized so that they can be transformed by the gospel of grace into the image of Jesus joining him in his mission to transform the world."[8] This is Derwin Gray's vision for evangelism at Transformation Church. After many years as an itinerant evangelist, Gray now concentrates on building a welcoming center for the lost and the least.

This is parallel to many awakenings, but none is so amazing as the little-known ministry of Aloys Henhöfer in southern Germany during the period of 1823–1862. He left his roots as a Catholic priest and established a revived church in Muhlhausen, a town near the Swiss border. From then

---

6. Matoga, www.facebook.com (accessed May 2, 2011).

7. Ibid.

8. Gray, email to author, October 5, 2011.

Emerging Awakening—A Faith Quake

on he traveled up and down the Rhine valley preaching and calling people to repentance. A power revival ensued, and it impacted southern Germany for more than 100 years.

During 1964 I was preaching in a small town named Sennfeld. As we sat in a farmhouse I noticed an old grandmother huddled near the stove. She called me over and gave this remarkable report: "A hundred years ago my father became a committed believer in Jesus. He urged us to pray for revival." Then she added this humbling phrase: "Now you have come, and revival has returned to our village." Revival has a passion for the lost.

Mark Driscoll expands on this concept. He challenges his congregation to be both a "sent and a sending church." He sees his listeners as missionaries scattered throughout the community to call people to living faith in Jesus Christ. Driscoll's declares it is his role to equip them for this evangelistic outreach.

This reminds me of the Indonesian Revival. During the late 1960s and early 1970s revival swept the island of Timor in Indonesia. One of my students was a missionary evangelist, and he reported upwards of three thousand conversions in one week. The Reformed Church Presbytery of Timor claimed that they had seen eighty thousand conversions in one year and after three years more than 200,000 had come to faith in Christ. The records of healings and miracles were amazing, and some people were actually raised from the dead.

One more emerging movement is notable. In London a church has sprung up among immigrants from Ghana and Nigeria. It is called Redeemed Church of God. These congregations typically have more than ten thousand or more worshipers. Into the numb spiritual atmosphere of postmodern and post-Christian England, the African evangelists have brought a new touch of spiritual life. When these churches combined for a night of prayer, more than forty thousand people turned up at the ExCel arena.

Revival is in the wind in Africa. It all began with the East Africa awakening in Rwanda and Uganda. Despite civil war and bloodshed this revival has grown and thrived eve since the 1920s. This movement has spread the joy of the indwelling Holy Spirit across East Africa, and it has become a fountainhead of revival not only for Africa, but also for the rest of the world.

Revival always reaps a harvest of souls. As Christ followers are ignited in their faith they reach out to friends and family members with the good news of the gospel. We are seeing this in unprecedented forms among the millennial believers, the emerging churches.

Changing the Cities

Revival across the history of Christianity has almost always been an urban phenomenon. This is also seen in the emerging movement, which has sprung up mainly in cities across the world. In our research we have found outbreaks across the United States from Mars Hill in Seattle to Elevation and Transformation in the Charlotte, North Carolina area. From City Church in New Haven, Connecticut to Sandals Church in Riverside, California. The same holds true when we look overseas. Kevin and Kerry Butterfield are ministering in Melbourne, Australia. International Christian Fellowship is found in Zurich, Switzerland, and Bristol City Center Church in in England. Hillsong has aimed at New York City for their American church plant.

One of the most unusual emerging churches is Christ Church London. It was born in the Strand Palace Hotel and five years later it had grown to six hundred each Sunday. In order to accommodate the crowd they have two services each Sunday at the Mermaid Theater in London. Peter Oborne explains: "The evangelical mission is enhanced by prayer groups that meet in homes, coffee shops, and restaurants across the capital."[9] It is a thoroughgoing city movement designed to reach the heart of London. It reminds me of the Fulton Street prayer meeting that launched a revival in New York in 1857. Office workers from across the city gravitated to the fish markets in Fulton Street for noontime prayer meetings (people who prayed were easily identified by the stench of fish). Before long their number outgrew the markets. Within a year similar revival prayer meetings had spread across the United States. Fulton Street is not far from Wall Street in the heart of Manhattan.

A second example of emerging city ministry is City Church in New Haven, Connecticut. The mission statement of City Church explains that the aim is "to spread the lifestyle of authentic Christianity to the glory of God and the transformation of our city."[10] The plain and prominent purpose of City Church is a total spiritual and economic and social revolution in the city. This reminds me of the work of John Wesley. In London he took over a disused foundry and renovated it into his first chapel. Located along City Road, this chapel was at the center of working class London. Here Wesley build a witness to reach the poor of the city, who flocked to the Methodist societies in droves. Across England Wesley also had an apartment and a

---

9. Oborne, "The Return to Religion."

10. This was from an unpublished handout from City Church in New Haven (July 2011).

chapel in the heart of Bristol. It is now open as a tourist site for Methodism. He worked his way across Bristol every day preaching on street corners and calling people to Christ. Wesley was passionate about reaching the cities.

A third example of urban ministry in the emerging church is Elevation Church in Charlotte, North Carolina. Steven Furtick, like Justin Kendrick, is open in his aim. He intends to see Elevation Church "dominate a city with the gospel of Jesus." Then he adds: "We can't think small. We will set impossible goals, take bold steps of faith, and watch God move."[11]

Let us draw one more comparison with revival movements. When Charles Haddon Spurgeon was called to a pulpit in London, he was a very young man, only twenty years old. He preached the church full in a short period of time and then moved his ministry to the great convention centers and public auditoriums. Spurgeon sometimes preached in other parts of England, but mainly he devoted his efforts to the transformation of London with the gospel. He was, so to speak, a man of one city.

Revival thrives best in cities. For this reason, the main preachers of the emerging movement are concentrating on cities around the world. During the 1960s and 1970s the American middle class abandoned the cities. One by one most cities became run down, crime infested, and dangerous. Now the millennial generation is reclaiming cities around the world for the gospel of Jesus Christ. This urban shift is one of the most satisfying and thrilling aspects of the emerging church movement. As the gospel is preached in cities revival springs up and the soul of the city is captured for Christ.

A Personal Epilogue

For most of my fifty years of ministry I have either preached in revivals or taught about revivals. To the glory of God alone I have been able to be a part of revivals in the Midwest during my childhood, in Germany during the first years of my preaching ministry, in England in the middle of my ministry, and most recently in China. Each revival is different. Culture shapes revival to the need of the time and the place. However, each revival is also similar. A passion for prayer and love for the lost and the least in society mark revival. It burns like fire as the Holy Spirit descends anew on the people of God.

During recent days I have visited and corresponded with revival leaders in the emerging movement. There is about these young leaders a

---

11. "Code of Elevation Church" as attached to Kim Villarreal's email to author, October 12, 2011.

Emerging Revival—Fact or Fantasy?

familiar feel of revival. They are driven by holy discontent with traditional religion. They are motivated to live missionally in the world. They are much more concerned with orthopraxy (faith alive) than they are with orthodoxy (doctrines believed.) They are determined to see the Holy Spirit descend in power on our world. As an older man I feel like Moses. I have been able to climb to the top of the mountain and see the promised land of revival. Like Caleb, the eighty-five year old hero of faith, I would love to be part of the conquest. Still, I know that time for me is ticking away. As my old friend Miss Jones put it: "I have seen the ocean waves of revival sweep over the land. Now the tide seems to be out, but the ocean is not empty." The emerging revival is truly a "faith quake."

Bibliography

"A Brief History of the Jesus Movement." *The Hollywood Free Paper* (2012). No pages. Online: http://www.hollywoodfreepaper.org/portal.php?id=2.

Aikman, David. *Jesus in Beijing: How Christianity is Transforming China and Changing the Global Balance of Power*. Washington, DC: Regnery, 2003.

Bell, Rob. *Love Wins: A Book About Heaven, Hell, and the Fate of Everyone Who Ever Lived*. New York: Harper One, 2011.

Boa, Kenneth D., and Robert M. Bowman, Jr. *Faith Has Its Reasons*. 2nd ed. Colorado Springs: Paternoster, 2001.

Cairns, Earle E. *Christianity Through the Centuries: A History of the Christian Church*. Revised and enlarged ed. Grand Rapids: Zondervan, 1981.

Calvary Chapel. "Our History." http://calvarychapel.com/index.php?option=com_content&view=article&id=49&Itemid=66.

Carson, D. A. *Becoming Conversant with the Emerging Church: Understanding a Movement and Its Implications*. Grand Rapids: Zondervan, 2005.

Chalke, Steve. *The Last Message of Jesus*. Grand Rapids: Zondervan, 2003.

Detzler, Wayne Alan. "British and American Contributions to the 'Erweckung' in Germany, 1815–1848." PhD diss., University of Manchester, 1974.

Detzler, Wayne Alan, and Douglas Potter. *Cross-Cultural Apologetics: Bridging Culture to Defend the Faith*. CreateSpace, 2011.

Driscoll, Mark. "Four Points of the Movement." Address presented at Resurgence, Orlando, FL, July 25, 2011.

———. "Just for Men." No pages. Online: http://theresurgence.com/files/2011/03/02relit_ebook_pac.pdf.

———. "Ten Painful Lessons from the Early Days of Mars Hill Church." Sermon, Mars Hill Church, Seattle, WA, December 6, 2011.

Driscoll, Mark, and Gary Breshears. *Vintage Jesus: Timeless Answers to Timely Questions*. Wheaton: Crossway Books, 2007.

Gibbs, Eddie. *I Believe in Church Growth*. London: Hodder and Stoughton, 1982.

———. *In Name Only: Tackling the Problem of Nominal Christianity*. Wheaton: Bridge Point, 1994.

Gibbs, Eddie, and Ryan Bolger. *Emerging Churches: Creating Christian Community in Postmodern Cultures*. Grand Rapids: Baker Academic, 2005.

Grudem, Wayne A. *Systematic Theology: An Introduction to Biblical Doctrine*. Grand Rapids: Zondervan, 1994.

Hyde, A. B. *The Story of Methodism Throughout the World*. Springfield, MA: Wiley, 1889.

Bibliography

Kendrick, Justin. "Building Foundations to Shake a City." Sermon at Frontier City Church, New Haven, CT, September 18, 2011.

Kinnaman, David. "Six Reasons Young Christians Leave Church." No pages. Online: http://www.barna.org/teens-next-gen-articles/528-six-reasons-young-christians-leave-church.

———. *You Lost Me: Why Young Christians are Leaving Church—and Rethinking Faith.* Grand Rapids: Baker, 2011.

Loizides, Lex. "John Wesley and William Wilberforce," *Church History Blog* (April 2010). No pages. Online: http://lexloiz.wordpress.com/2010/04/05/john-wesley-and-william-wilberforce.

McKnight, Scot. "Five Streams of the Emerging Church." *Christianity Today* (June 2011). No pages. Online: http://www.christianitytoday.com/ct/2007/february/11.35.html.

———. *The Jesus Creed: Loving God, Loving Others.* Brewster, MA: Paraclete, 2004.

McLaren, Brian. *A Generous Orthodoxy: Why I am Missional, Evangelical, Post/Protestant, Liberal/Conservative, Mystical/Poetic, Biblical, Charismatic/Contemplative, Fundamentalist/Calvinist, Anabapist/Anglican, Methodist, Catholic, Green, Incarnational, Depressed-Yet-Hopeful, Emergent, Unfinished Christian.* Grand Rapids: Zondervan, 2004.

National Leadership Council. "Core Values." http://www.nps.gov/training/uc/tcv.htm.

Nee, Watchman. *The Normal Christian Life.* Radford, VA: Wilder, 2008.

Oborne, Peter. "The Return to Religion." *The Daily Telegraph* (Jan. 1 2012). No pages. Online: http:// www.telegraph.co.uk/news/religion/8970031/The-return-to-religion.

Rienecker, Fritz. *Sprachlicher Schluessel zum Griechischen Neuen Testament.* 10th ed. Giessen-Basel: Brunnen, 1960.

The Resurgence. "Resurgence: A Ministry of Mars Hill." www.theresurgence.com.

Tickle, Phyllis. *The Great Emergence: How Christianity Is Changing and Why.* Grand Rapids: Baker, 2008.

Tucker, Ruth A. *Parade of Faith—A Biographical History of the Christian Church.* Grand Rapids: Zondervan, 2011.

Warfield, B. B. *Counterfeit Miracles.* Edinburgh: Banner of Truth, 1972.

Wesley, John. "The Conversion of John Wesley." http://www.forthegospel.org/articles/the_conversion_of_john_wesley.

Zschech, Darlene. *Extravagant Worship.* Grand Rapids: Bethany House, 2002.

———. *The Great Generational Transition.* San Francisco: EWI, 2009.

———. *Kiss of Heaven.* Grand Rapids: Bethany House, 2003.

———. *Worship.* Sydney: Hillsongs, 1996.

www.ingramcontent.com/pod-product-compliance
Lightning Source LLC
Chambersburg PA
CBHW071857160426
43197CB00013B/2514